TREADWELL

PREFACE BY MARIA MORRIS HAMBOURG

ESSAY BY E. ANNIE PROULX

PHOTOGRAPHS BY ANDREA MODICA

TREADWELL

A CONSTANCE SULLIVAN BOOK

CHRONICLE BOOKS, SAN FRANCISCO

Printed in the United States of America

Library of Congress Cataloging-in-Publication Data:
Modica, Andrea.
Treadwell; photographs by Andrea Modica;
preface by Maria Morris Hambourg; essay by E. Annie Proulx.
p. cm.
ISBN 0-8118-1118-2
1. Portrait photography. 2. Modica, Andrea. I. Proulx, Annie.
II.Title.
TR680.M63 1996
779'.'24'092–dc20 95–34059
CIP

Prints courtesy of Julie Saul Gallery, New York City.

Distributed in Canada by Raincoast Books
8680 Cambie Street
Vancouver, B.C. V6P 6M9

10 9 8 7 6 5 4 3 2 1

Chronicle Books
275 Fifth Street
San Francisco, CA 94103

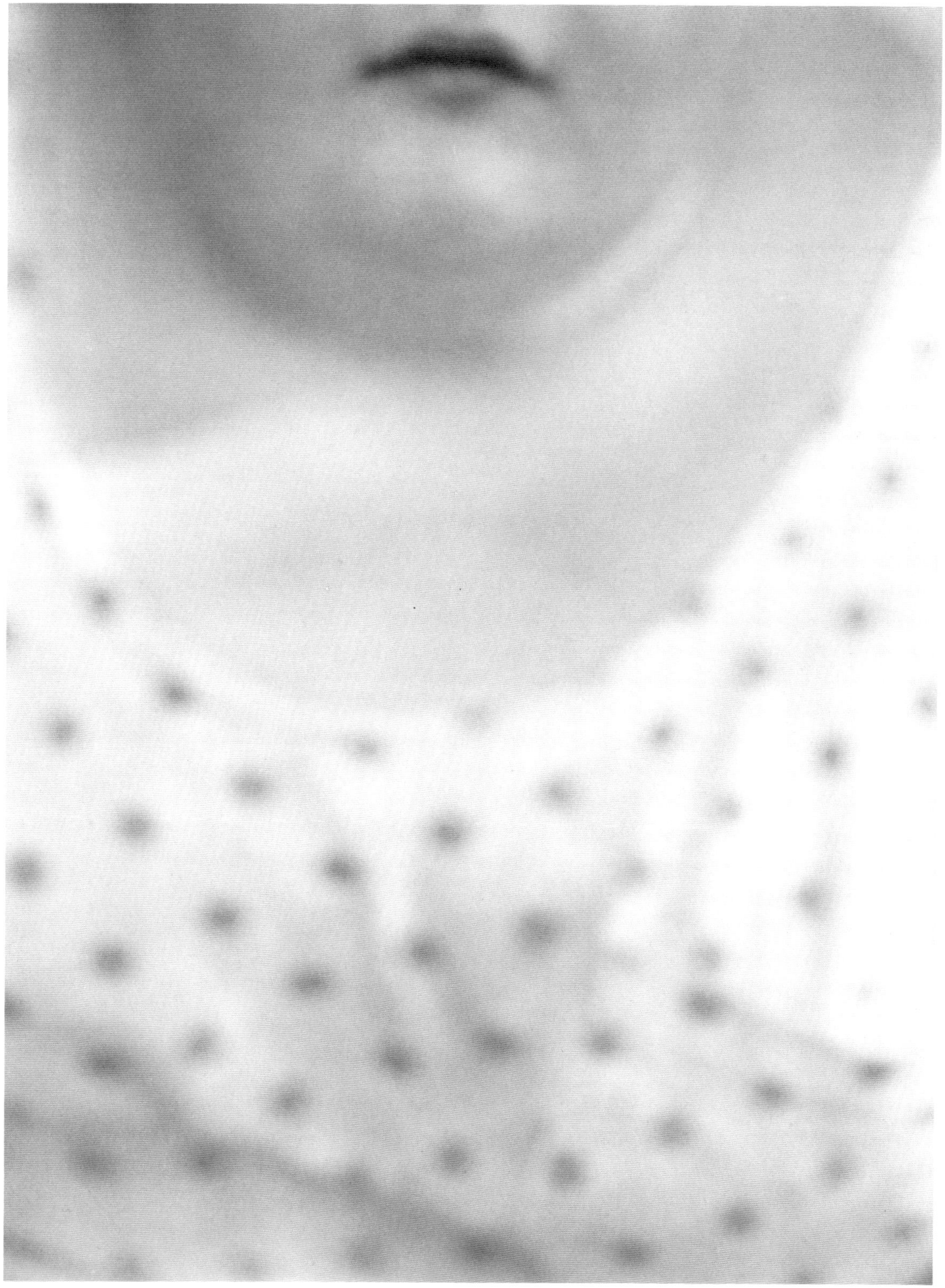

PREFACE

MARIA MORRIS HAMBOURG

THIS BOOK IS NOT ABOUT TREADWELL, NEW YORK. Except for the first plate, the photographs were not made there but in a dozen or more forgettable locations. Some people depicted here never met their "neighbors" on the next page, adjacent scenes are sometimes separated by years, and seamed into the seedy rural weave of the book are slices of an urban space. Like Faulkner's Jefferson County, Treadwell is a place in the imagination, a name and a frame to contain the artist's story.

The artist, Andrea Modica, was born in Brooklyn of Italian parentage. She was raised a Catholic and had the good fortune of being taught morality and compassion more than mores and catechism. The texts were from the Bible, but the memorable examples were straight from life. In college she studied art and art history and was drawn to the formal rigor of Egypt and the human drama of Italian painters such as Caravaggio. She tried painting, which she found "too loose," and for a time she thought the structural necessity of sculpture was the answer. In the end she elected the camera.

Photography offered Modica "something technical to hold on to," formulae and fixed limits to begin from, to master, and soon to work against. Within the bounds of its procedures she found the freedom to sculpt meticulous, sensuous pictures. The 8 x 10-inch view camera she shoulders is cumbersome and deliberate; it "stacks the deck" against facility. It also provides negatives large enough to describe fine textures such as flesh without disintegrating into grain.

Modica's art is about important and solemn events—those internal, molding moments we are mostly powerless to hold or to articulate. Modica seized such a moment with Barbara in

1986 (page 15), and although she has turned her camera on other subjects in the past decade, this beautiful plump child became her touchstone to revisit over the years, and, eventually, the main character of this picture story.

At the outset of the story we witness the power of vision: the emotions elicited in the observant child as she relates to events outside her disclose her sensitivity and establish the moral climate of "Treadwell." The artist then paints the landscape and the rites and mysteries of its local tribe—the animal spirits they worship, defame, and sacrifice. We see how close to nature these people are, how they interact with each other, and then, as their culture matures, how they become conscious and project images of themselves. They elaborate their embodiments with cosmetics and devise more complex rituals using scarification, masks, and icons.

Towards the end of the story, the scene changes to a sacramental realm where transformation, death, and spiritual grace may enter, or be revealed as make-believe. Modica leaves us here where the imagination reigns because that is where she lives—the domain of art, the artist's home. *Treadwell* is a fiction about a little girl growing up. It is also a history of art and an autobiography.

RELIQUARY

E. ANNIE PROULX

THERE IS A TREADWELL, POPULATION 200, in rural New York south of the Susquehanna, south of Interstate 88, and it is the place where, ten years ago, Andrea Modica took the first and now famous photograph in this study, two children caught in the hands of adults; we look and wonder, are they sheltered or imprisoned, resigned or straining against the hold, is the clasp tender, is the bathrobed child prevented from hearing something dreadful, is the other seeing something that can never be forgotten? The slant of white buttons, the tiny downward glint of a ring introduces us to the richly fleshed and beautiful child who is the central figure in *Treadwell*, moving from this moment out of childhood toward the shoals of adult life.

In 1986 Andrea Modica was a young photographer just up from Brooklyn, stunned, she says, by the dark of the rural hinterland, the light in winter short and strained through cloud, in summer filtered through heavy leaf. The interiors of houses seemed enfolded, drenched in shadow. "This picture was a turning point for me," she says, leaning forward, her elbow on the table. "Until this one I had been photographing in a place that was like a foreign country to me—photographing like a tourist." But with this picture she entered into an intimacy with the situation of place, the chewed-over woods and fields of central New York State, the region's moody, autumnal weather, the rural slowing of time that is like wading through backwater, and began a kind of episodic story in photographs that the viewer pieces together.

The photographs do not illustrate the real Treadwell of Delaware County but offer us enigmatic and portentous moments of people in constricting rural circumstances in a late decade of this troubled century. Modica glances across the table at her box of platinum prints and says, "reliquaries."

'Reliquary' is a curious word to describe a photograph, for in its strict meaning a reliquary is a small box or casket in which one keeps or exhibits relics. And 'relic' is itself a word of complex meanings: a corpse; bodily fragments of saints; the bits and pieces left after the disintegration of a group of people; surviving objects that serve as memorial to an individual, souvenirs, mementos. Whose relics? For the young girl who is the central focus of these photographs, they may serve as relics of a childhood; for Modica they may represent fragments of a place, people and a time in her eye's life; for the viewer the images may fall into an interior reliquary of secret personal experiences and memories. The sense of reliquary is sharply illustrated in the photograph (page 63) where a child holds out a shallow cardboard box in which repose two socks stiff with grime, on one cuff a bit of hanging lace, the lace torn away from the other, crusty with dirt and stretched shapeless, yet a relic of, and ironic comment on, girlish dainties—a reliquary within a reliquary.

For a decade Modica followed her subjects from one decayed farmhouse to another, photographing in an atmosphere of crowded rooms and generations of lost chances and bad luck. The photographs are not some chronicle of despair, but caught moments in lives ruled by hard situations; there are possibilities of anything. Because the photographs follow a timeline the viewer cannot help but construct a narrative. There is a beginning, a flow of events and episodes, the children grow older, sexual tension increases, lipstick is smeared, caries eat at the teeth, a finger points. Yet the unknown possibilities triumph; in the last two photographs a child drives somewhere imaginary in a wrecked car, and the muddy road curves outward, away from whatever lies behind the photographer.

Modica has a strong eye for the human condition. We are able to catch telling pieces of lives in a single photograph, glimpse private intimacies, animal pleasure, the comfort of skin. She sees, and shows us how to see, a kind of beauty in mean lives, the beauty of affection and gesture, of imaginative play, even with such a macabre object as a decaying fawn head—relic of deer, of hunt, of deed.

There is a sculptural, heroic quality in many of these photographs. They feel large. They possess a tactile physicality. Often the images of the children are like fantastic statues in some wild garden. There is a sense of beating, scratching life, of inchoate longing and suppressed anger. A taut classical pose of two children (page 15) vibrates off the page with energy, the grotesque bound and bag-headed figure (page 59) metamorphoses in our minds from Halloween dress-up to the figure of a seer silenced, or the approaching hour for a ritual murder. The ancient lotus posture of a little girl (page 77) is saturated with meaning beyond her culture. The sculptural effect seems heightened by the outlandish clothes of the late twentieth century, sagging knit fabrics emblazoned with logos and mottoes. Do we see Laocoön in writhing bodies (page 68), or, in the myriad folds of a dirty blanket (page 69), do we see the girl molting from some huge rough skin, or do we feel a Japanese quality of crumpled silk metamorphosing into a cascade of mountain water?

Throughout, parts of bodies, arms, hands, legs and feet, a mound of belly, the swell of cheek and knee, a severed head, wet fur of dead muskrats, tufts of hair, fragments of events, come to us like curls of ash flying up from a bonfire of pages, a few achingly enigmatic words, but all that we have of the story. One of the most striking photographs (page 55) is a composition of triangles setting off an obese arm marred with inked claw marks, self-inflicted mock mutilation. The arm rests on another arm, that of the torn and grimed chair, the back of the hand falls lax on the scabby windowsill, the palm half-open, the fingers curled loosely. In other pictures an arm stretches down from a bed; a hand emerges from the shadows to grip a twisted sapling behind a sullen adolescent whose mouth is bruised with leafshadow; a twist of wind-blown curtain like an extended arm and rigid finger points at a jack-knifed body. Sometimes the arm is only a rigid bar of light piercing the composition, sometimes it is a warning, the admonitory or commanding hand, or the hand on early gravestones pointing the way, or the revealing hand showing us what we must know.

There are a number of pictures in *Treadwell* reminiscent of cenotaphs and nineteenth-century memorial photographs of the dead. The sheet over the window (page 73) might be marble, and so might the child's figure silent on its stone pillow, the eyelids weighted, not with pennies, but with postage stamps torn from an envelope. The child in clench-mouthed sleep (page 79) looks as though it has been cast down from a cliff, and the disclosing hand—behold!—drawing aside the curtain, shows us not only the abandoned body but ourselves in the common recognition of the quilt pattern of manufactured bedding, shows us crumpled socks as husks of body parts with the life force emptied out of them.

The child playing in the satellite dish hole (page 81) is also reminiscent of the graveyard. Among the detritus of rural life we see a child who seems to be pretending resurrection from an opened grave, the rectangle of chipboard a tombstone thrown aside.

Quite different from these deathly images, and oddly sensual in tone, is the woman sitting cross-legged and holding a rat-haired child (page 43), in the background another woman-and-child, all in a ravaged landscape of sawdust, bark rinds and waste slabs from a sawmill operation. The woman's feral face, the raw sawyard, give the scene the feel of a traveler's photograph of some chance encounter in another century.

There are strong contrasts of values in these photographs, not only of chiaroscuro and light, but of the tender flesh of children in contact with coarse, raspy grass, with brambles, flesh shown against bark and waste wood or dead leaves, stones and gravel, human junk. One of the most jarring images in *Treadwell* (page 75), shows a little girl in incongruous flounces kneeling on a stained mattress, and in the shadow of her body the light catches the white pencils of her fingers; if we look further—nothing is overt in Modica's sly photographs—we see the babyish hands grip and aim a handgun.

Among the richest photographs—in the sense of submerged story—are the lovers in the grass (page 19), the suspended deer's head (page 30), the skeleton of the horse (page 29). These deep-layered photographs have the power of allegory.

The oblivious lovers in the cold grass, the bleak landscape, the wreck of junk, the asphalt shingle that covers the clapboards of an old farmhouse, the glaring window, all are eclipsed by the extraordinary expression on the face of the watching child. She stares fixedly at the straining lovers as she hoists a grimacing cat, her expression a mixture of nascent longing, tenderness, curiosity, a sense of intrusion, recognition of the existence of heated passion. She becomes any child in any time recognizing the sexual act which lies in her future.

The suspended deer head, eyes closed, long neck attached, seems simple enough at first glance, a successful hunt (in fact a young boy's first deer), but the more we look the more we see. It is not usual to hang a deer by the neck. Rather, they are commonly suspended from a gambrel with the muzzle toward the ground for bleeding out. In the picture the rope is thin and frazzled, in fact, it is not a rope at all but a length of binder twine which could not support the weight of a deer. The head, then, is a trophy, hung up after the venison was cut into joints and chops; the inanimate tree begins to take on a morbid color. On the left face of the tree a barely visible POSTED sign warns trespassers from hunting on the property. We see that the tree is part of a boundary line marked by a slovenly barbed wire fence. At the base of the tree on the right lie a few short boards, and overhead, the stub of a branch, sawed, perhaps. The branches of an apple tree extend into the picture. We guess, then, that deer come to this place to eat windfall apples, that the boards on the ground were part of a crude ladder (replaced by new boards that we cannot see?) nailed to the tree; access to a hunter's tree stand. That branch stub has surely been sawed to open a line of vision to feeding deer. Now we understand that the tree plays a major role in the death of deer. Below the tree is a rabbit cage with the door standing open, and scattered over the ground among patches of early snow, are great tufts of deer hair as though the hide of the animal had been torn apart by fangs.

In another, the skeleton of a horse lies in the dead leaves as it fell, surrounded by a mazy thicket of saplings. We stare and see the hooves still standing, eerily upright, like a spare set the skeleton may use some moony night. Just past the gaping nasal cavity a twist of plastic seems its frozen last breath. And there beyond the saplings, as though risen from the bones, is that a ghost horse, an after-image of life, a reincarnation, a dream-animal, or another fragment in the reliquary of *Treadwell*?

These pictures were made in upstate New York between 1986 and 1995.

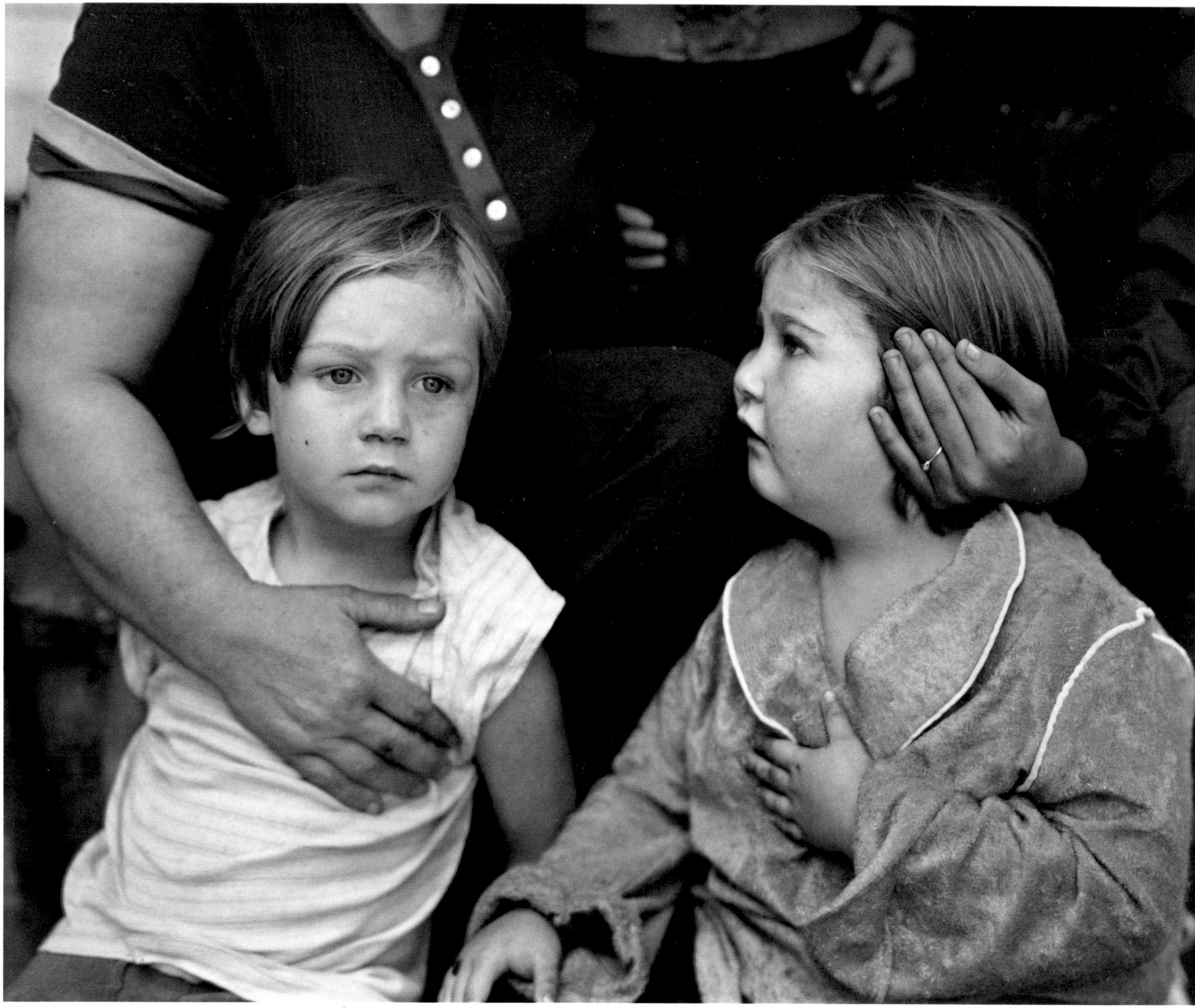

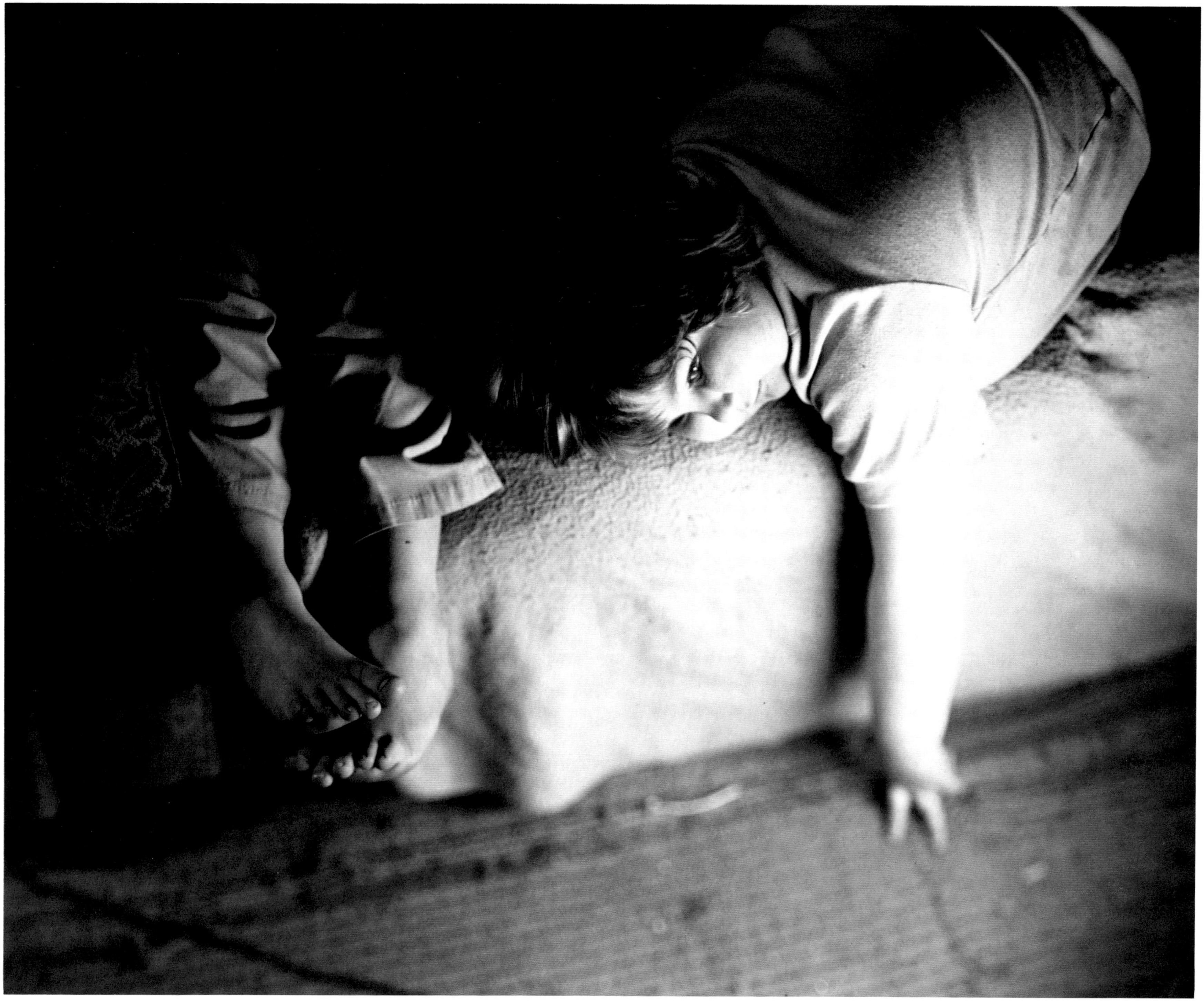

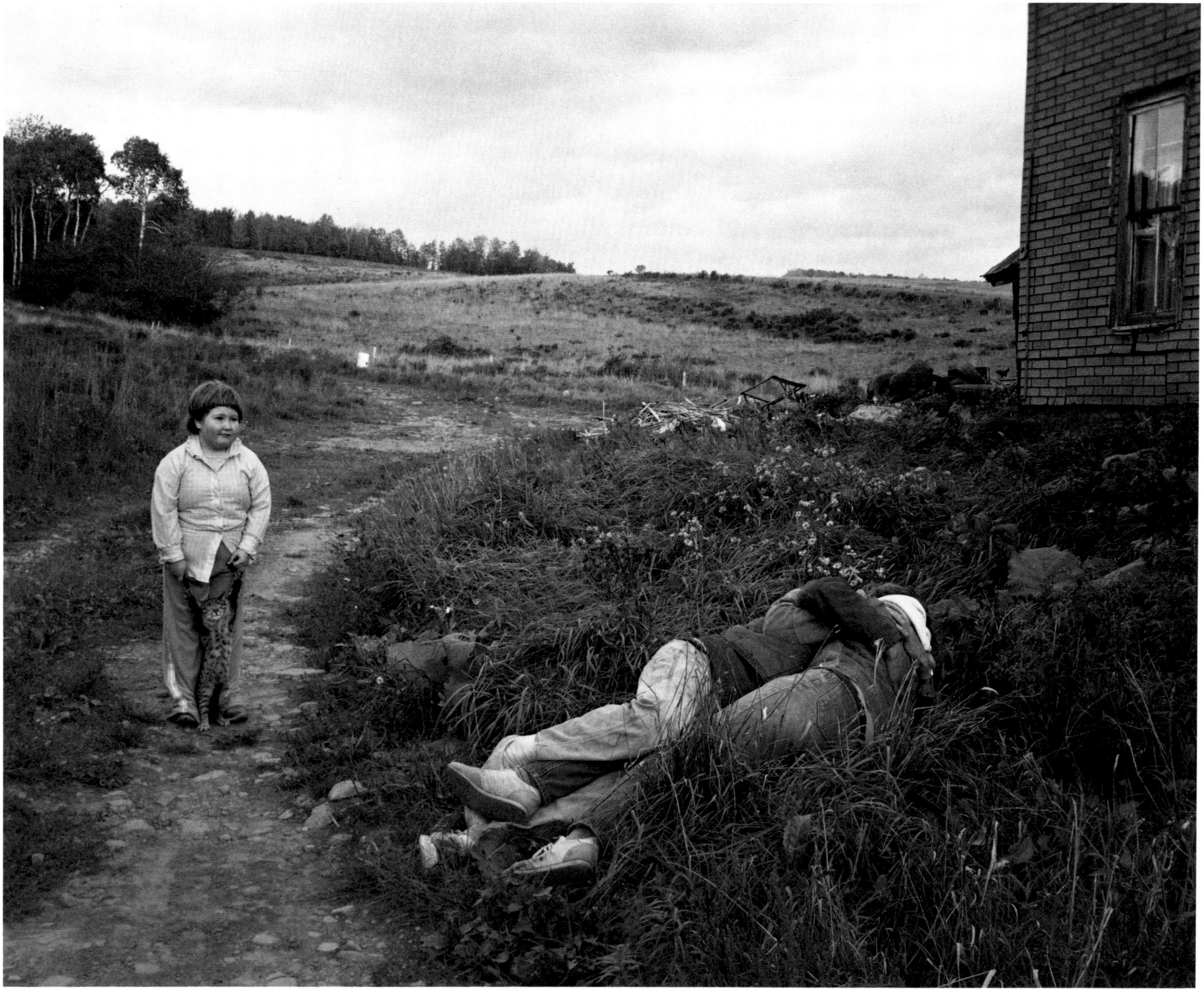

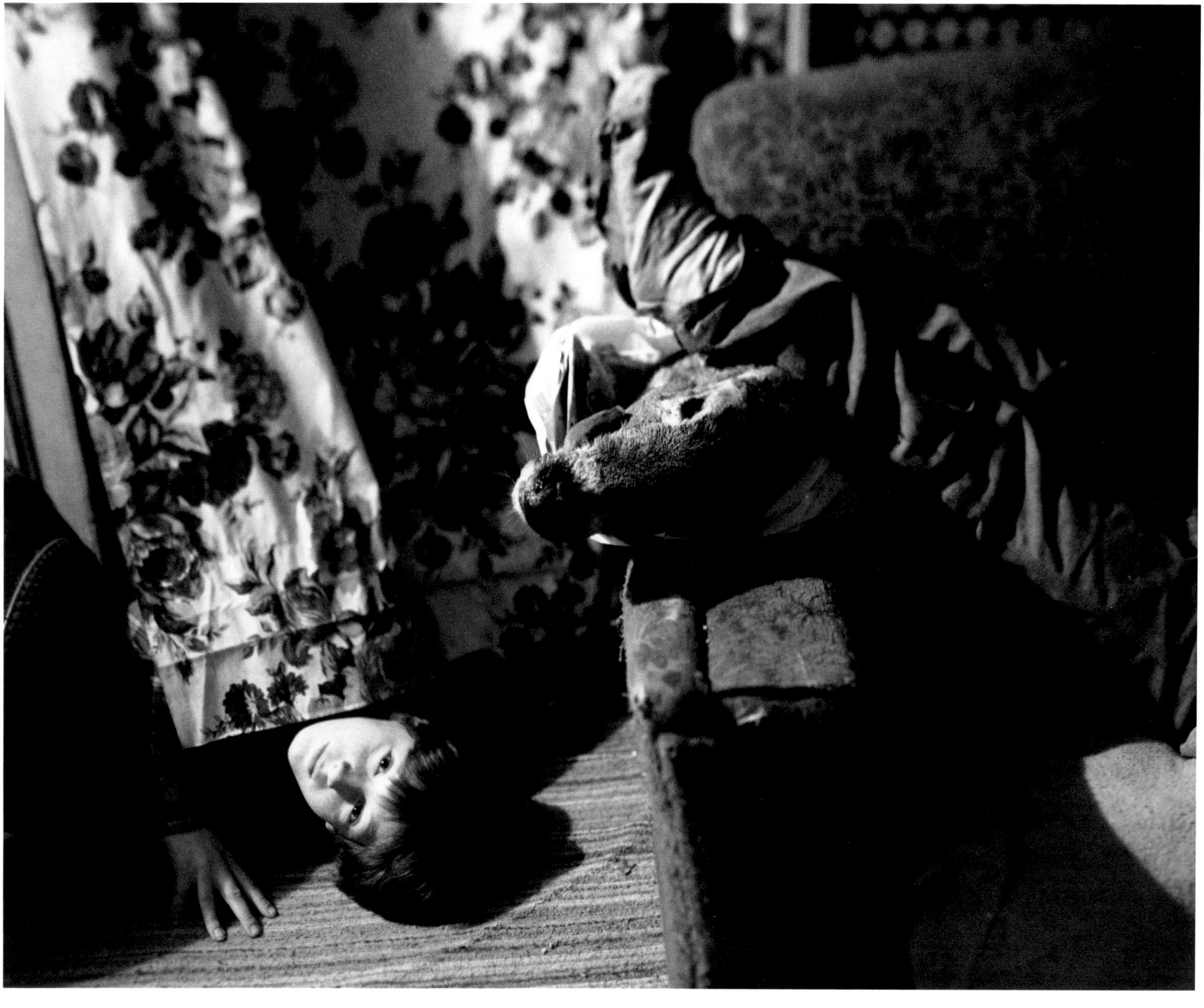

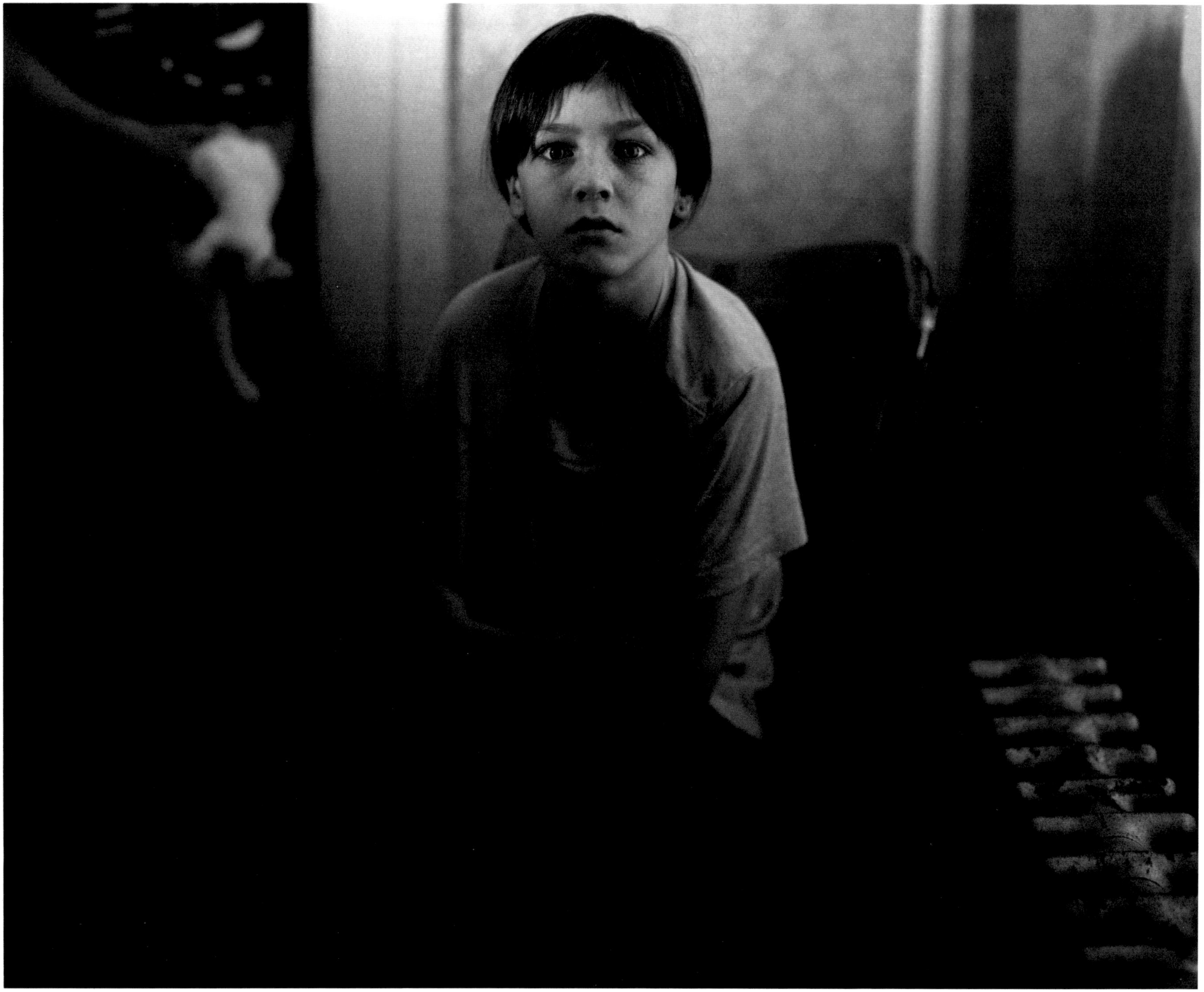

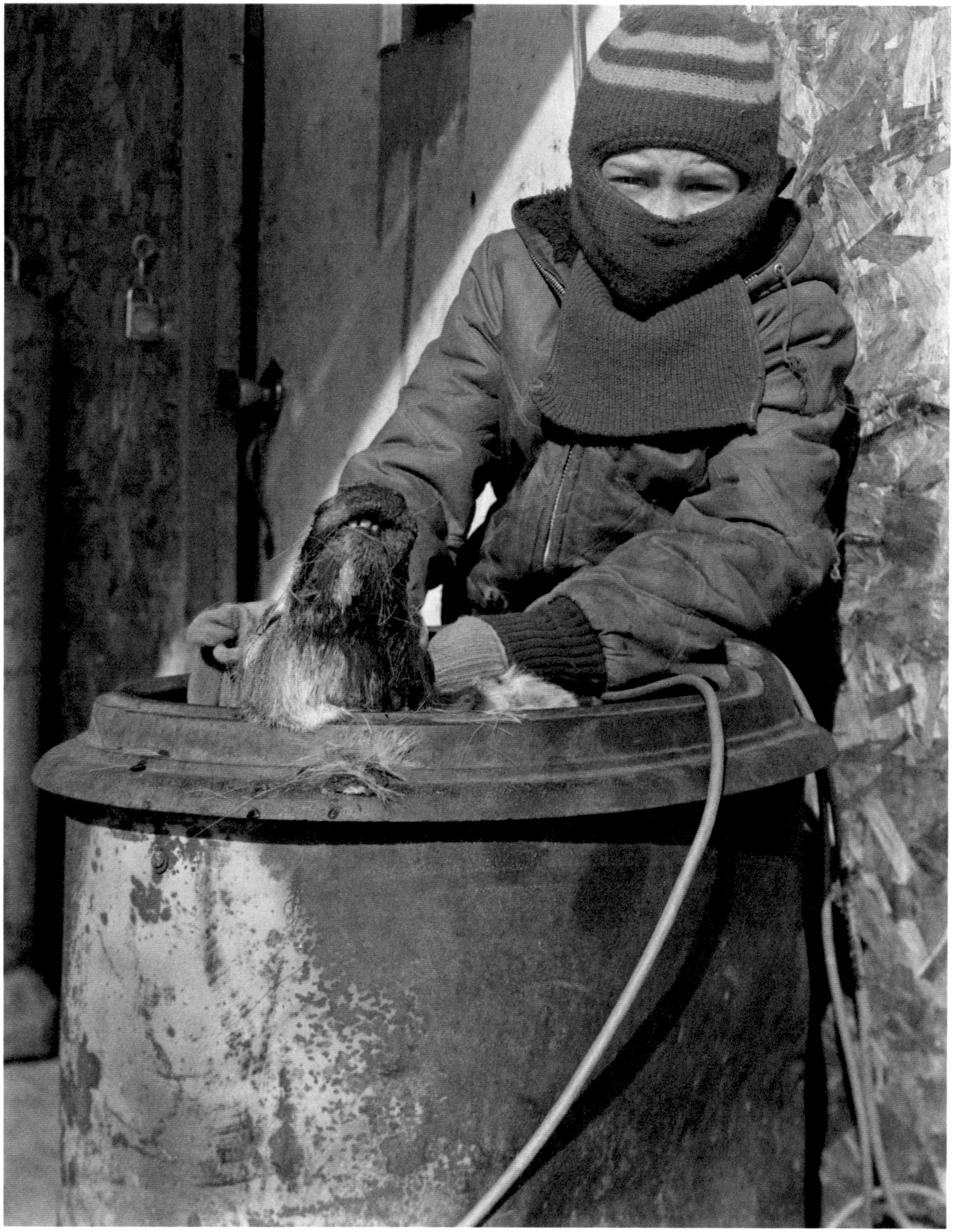

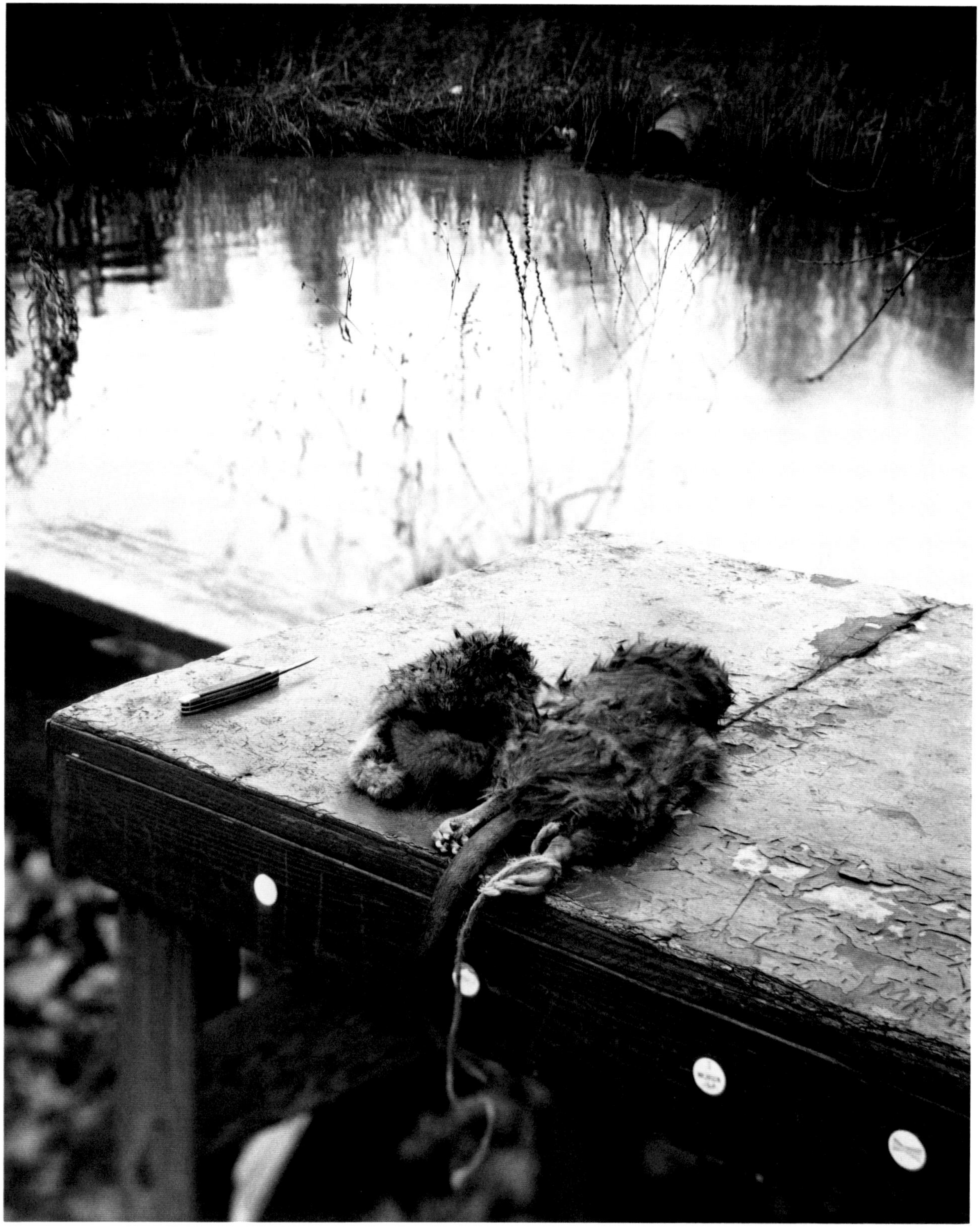

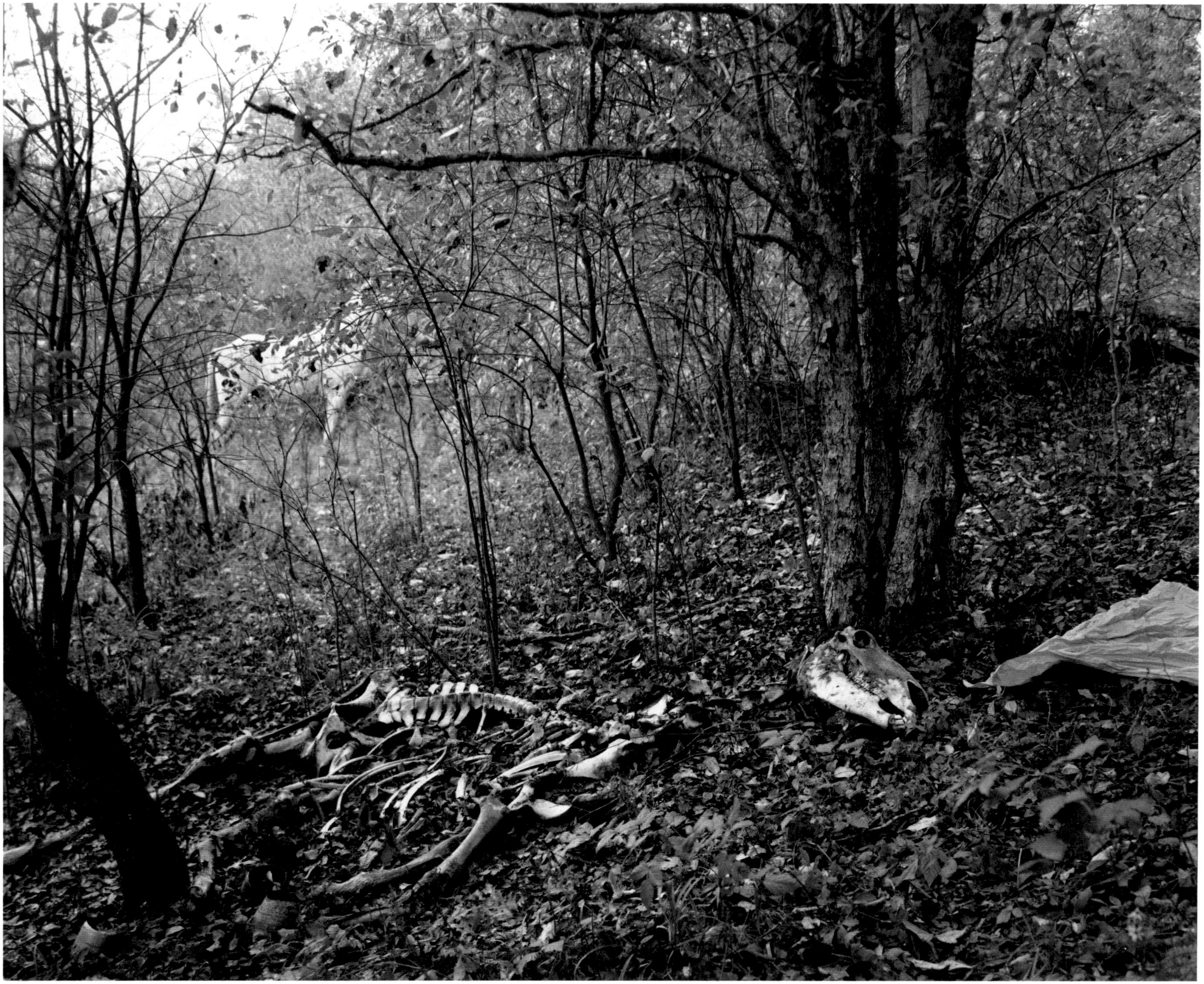

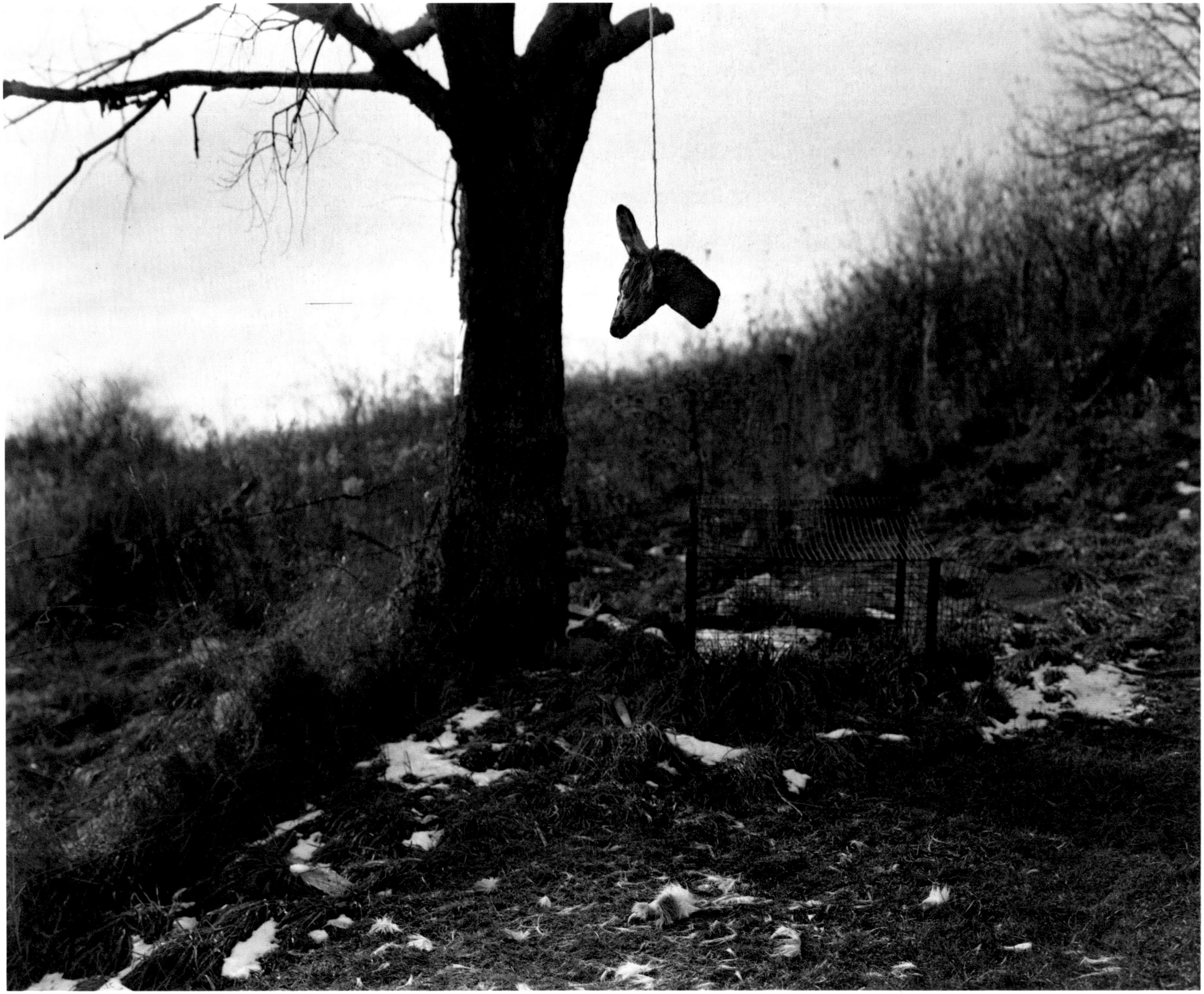

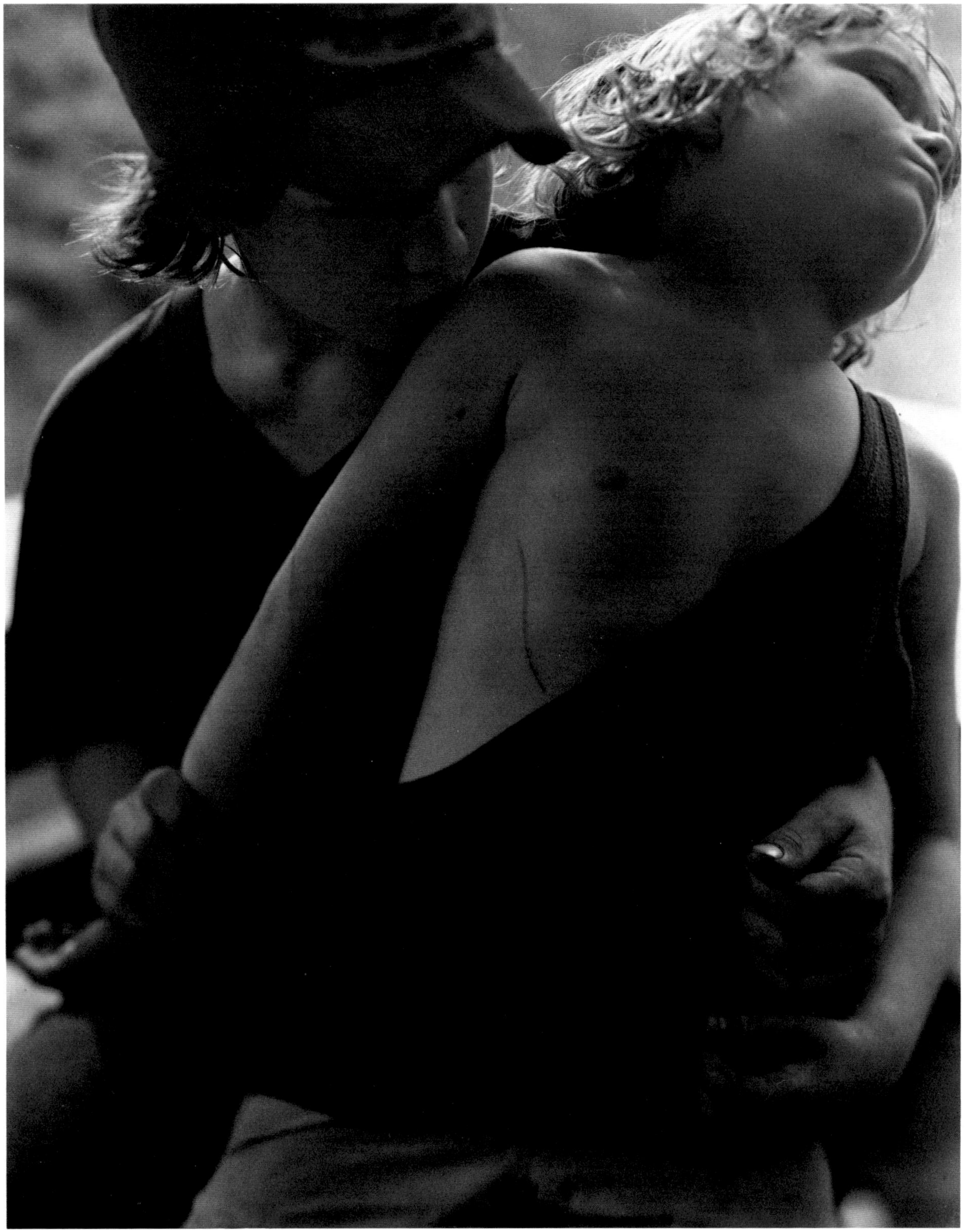

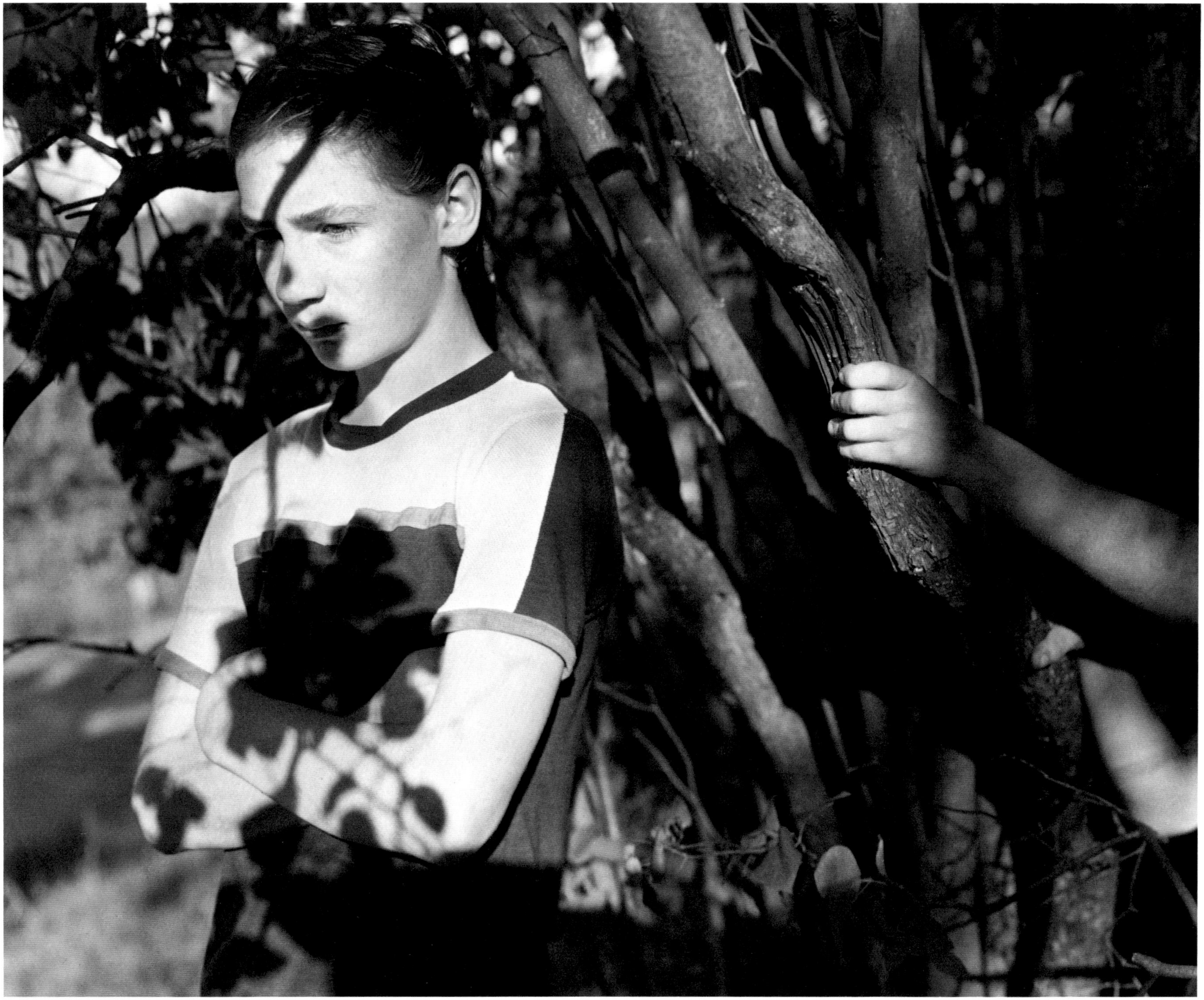

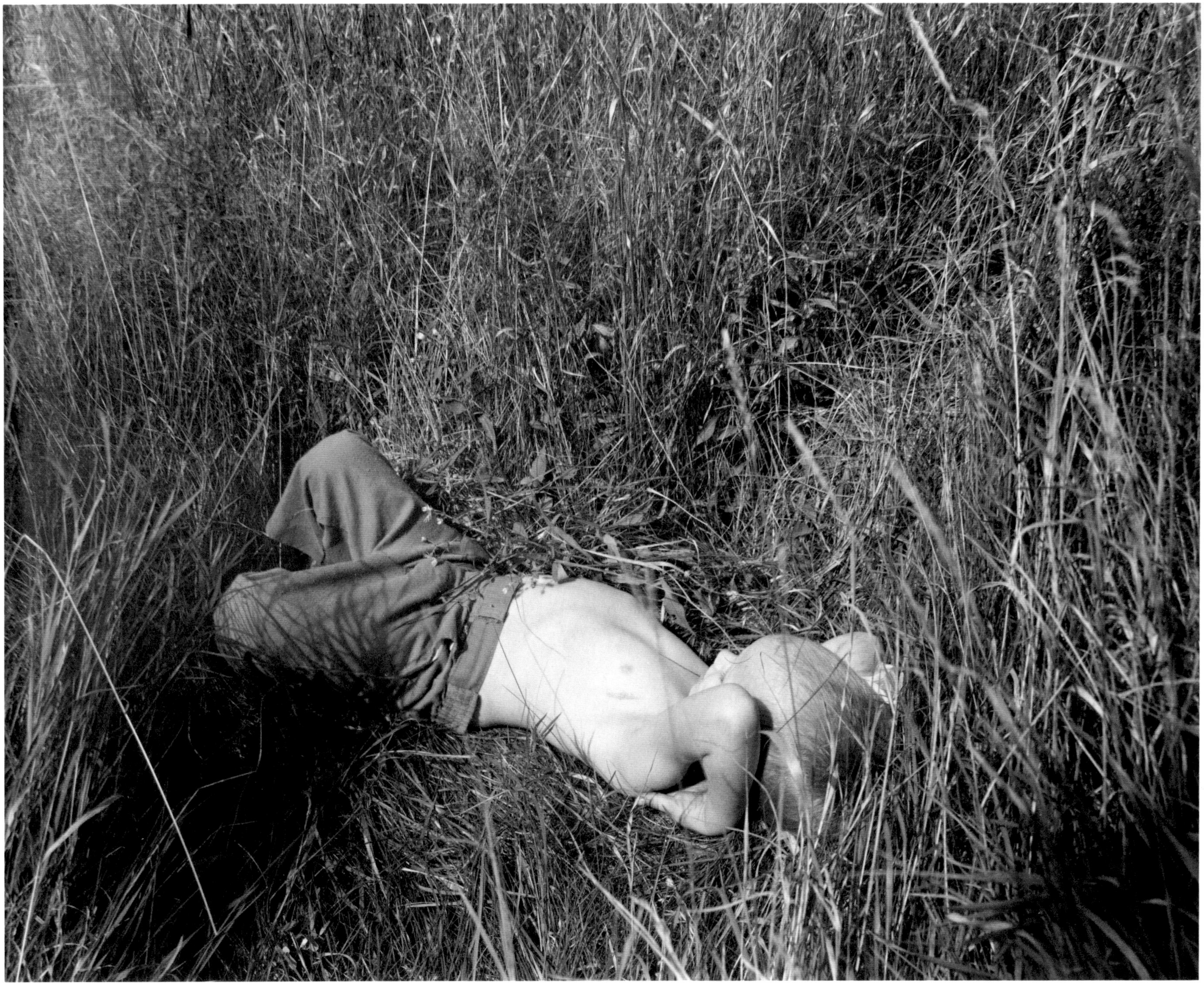

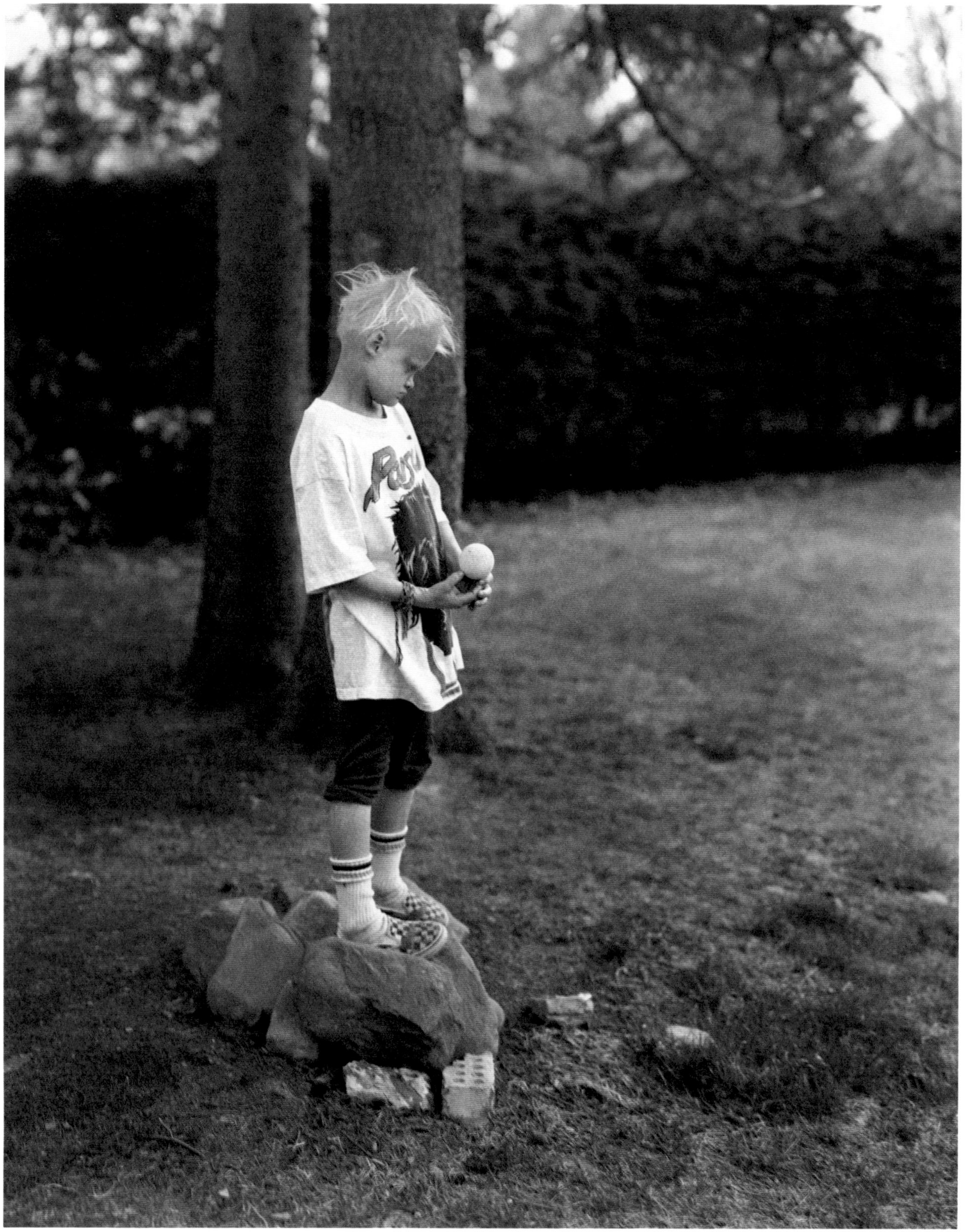

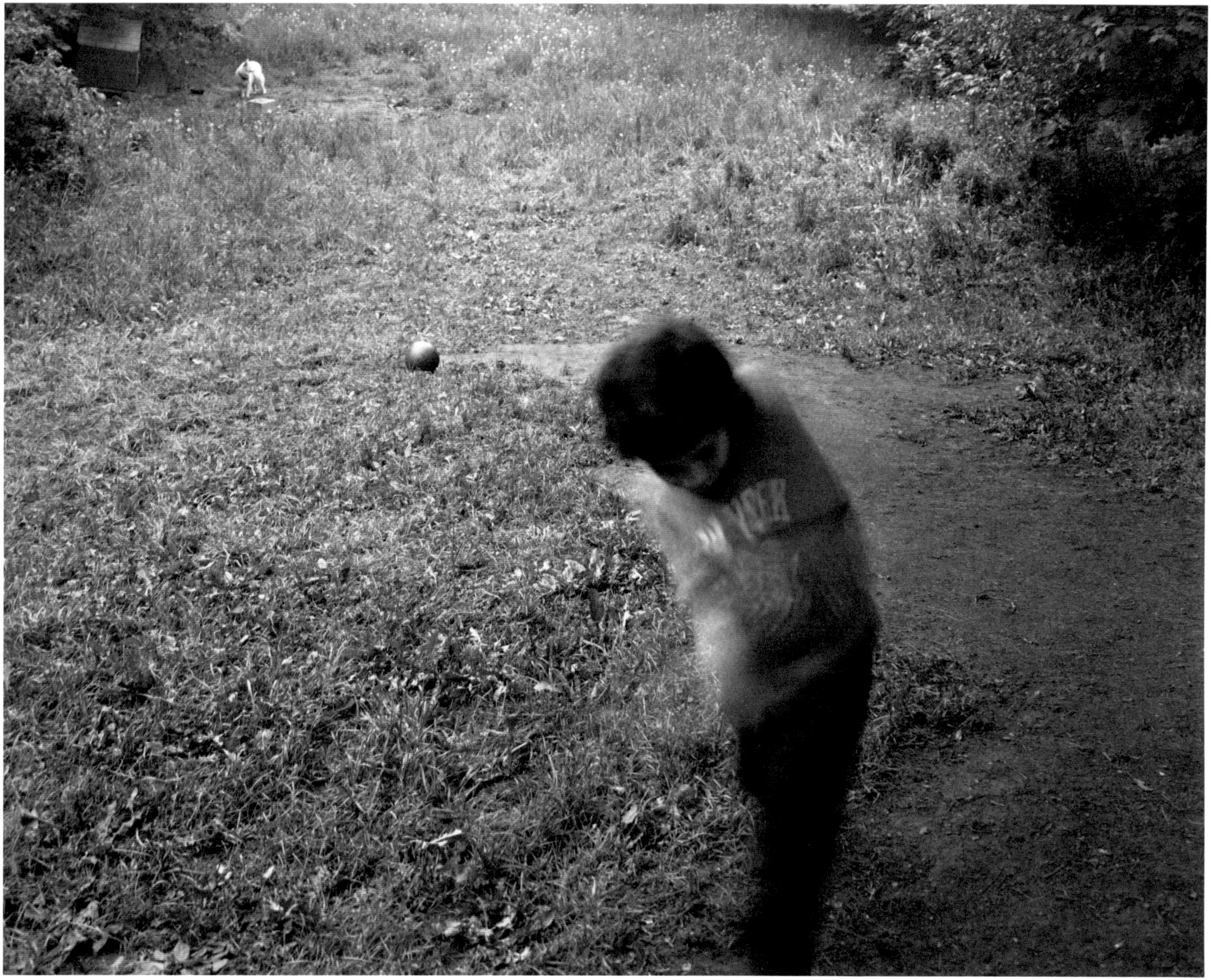

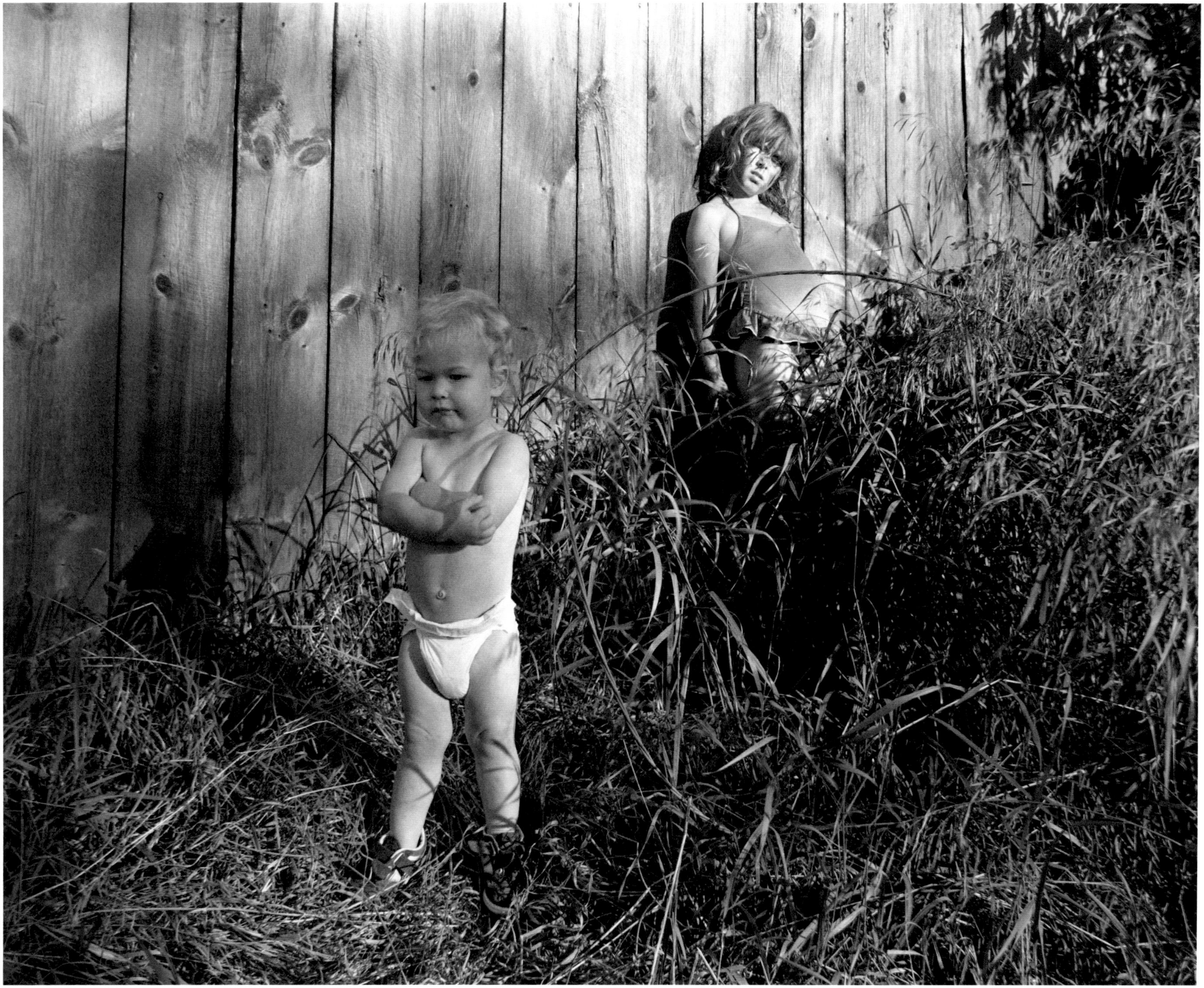

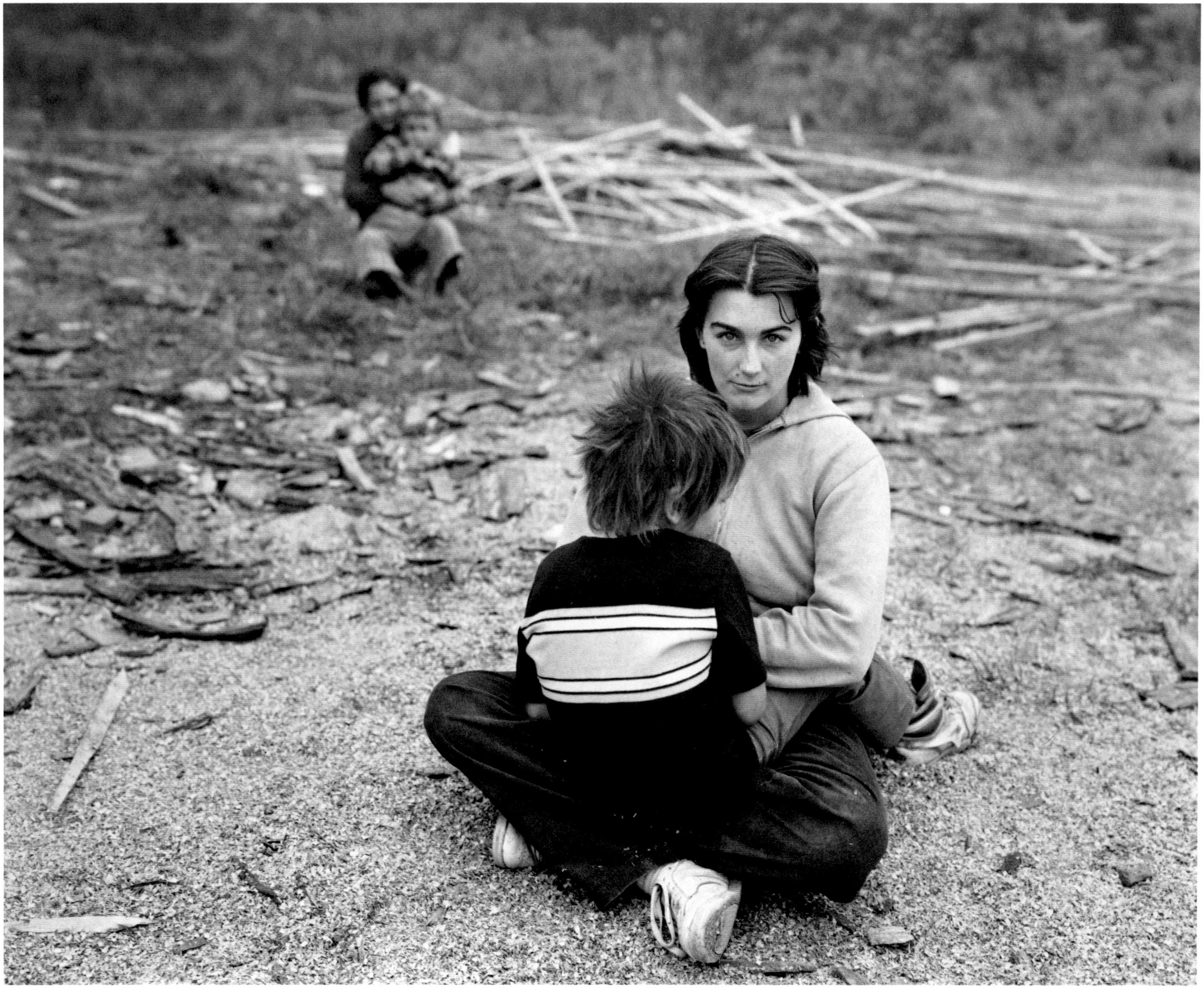

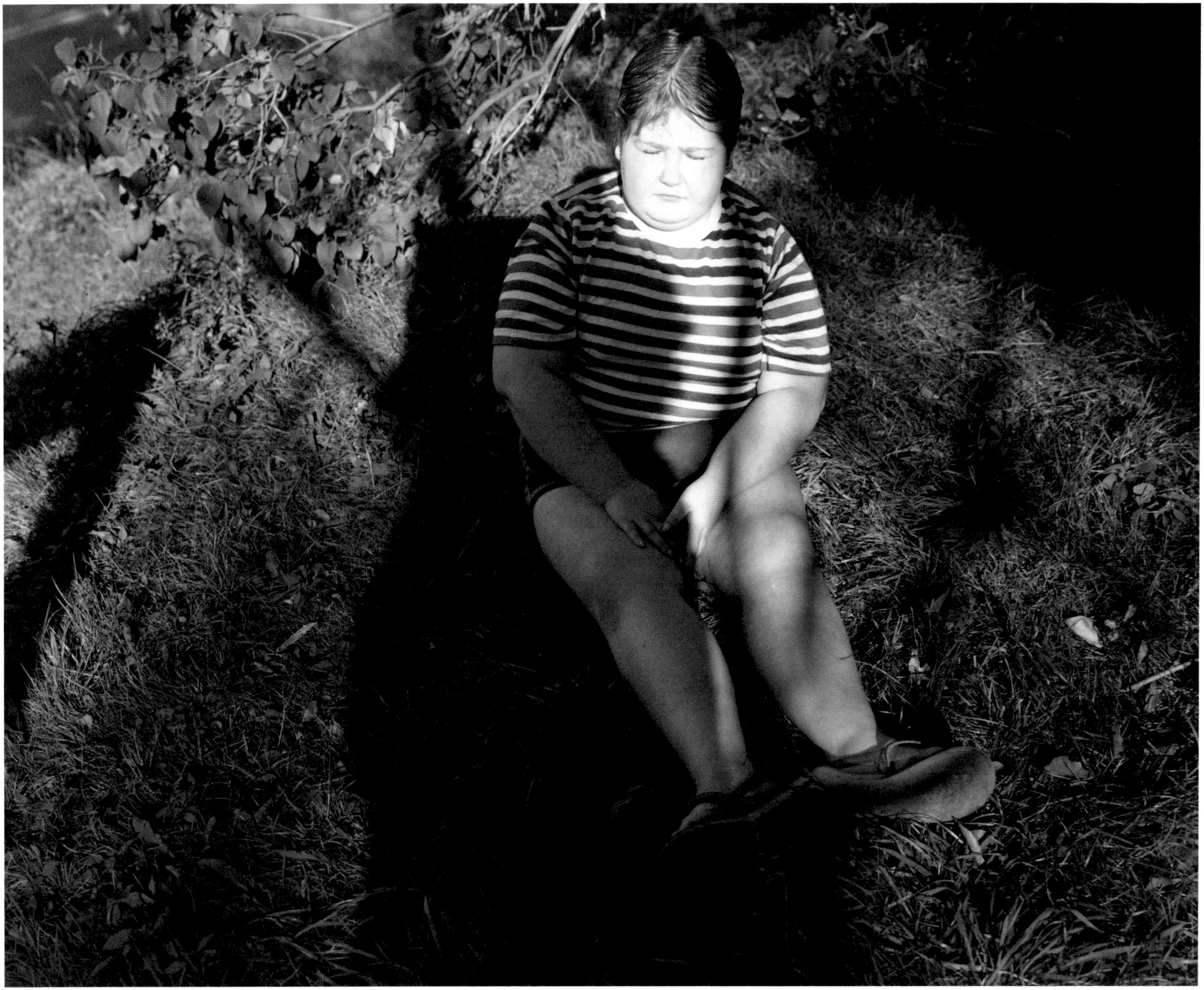

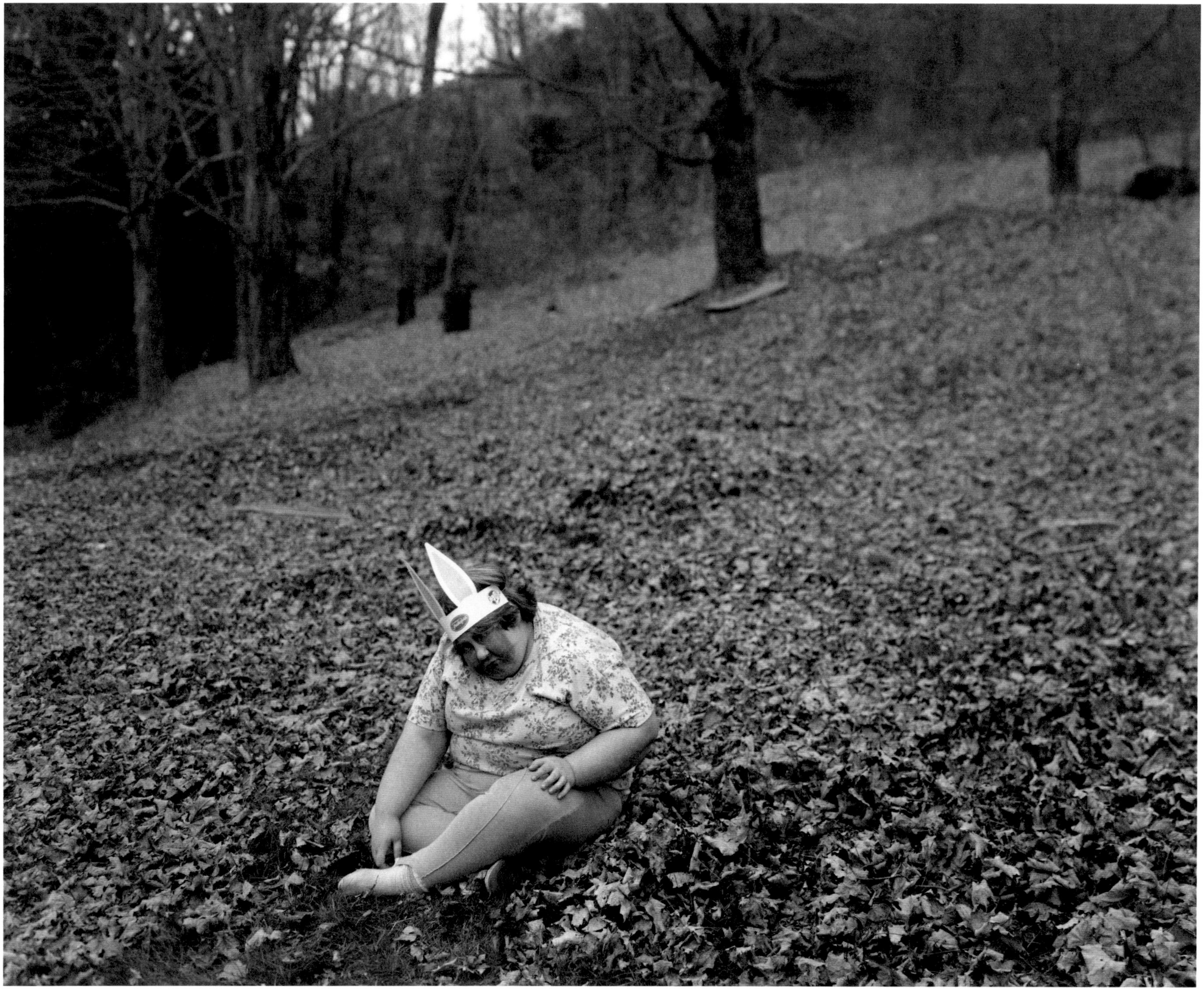

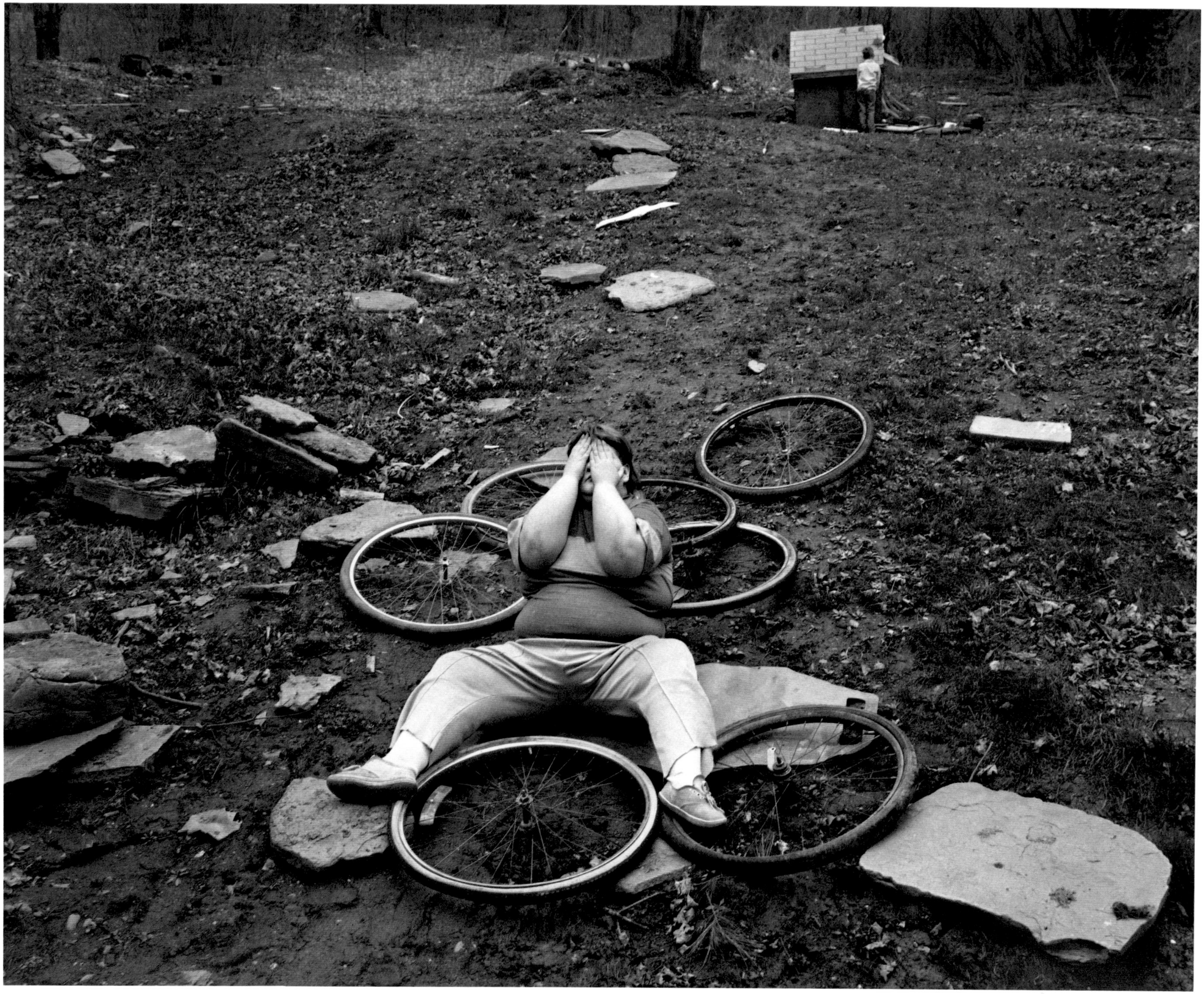

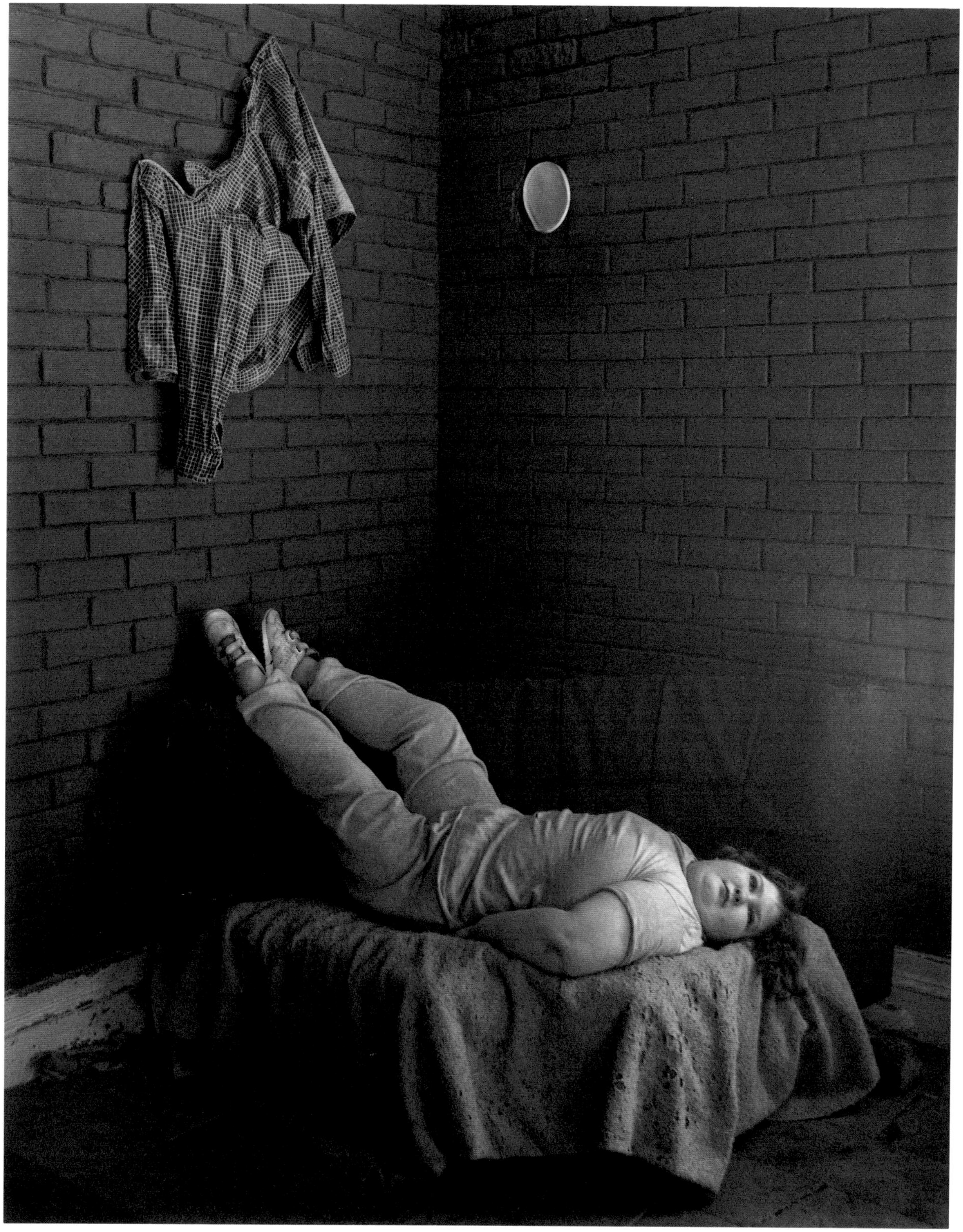

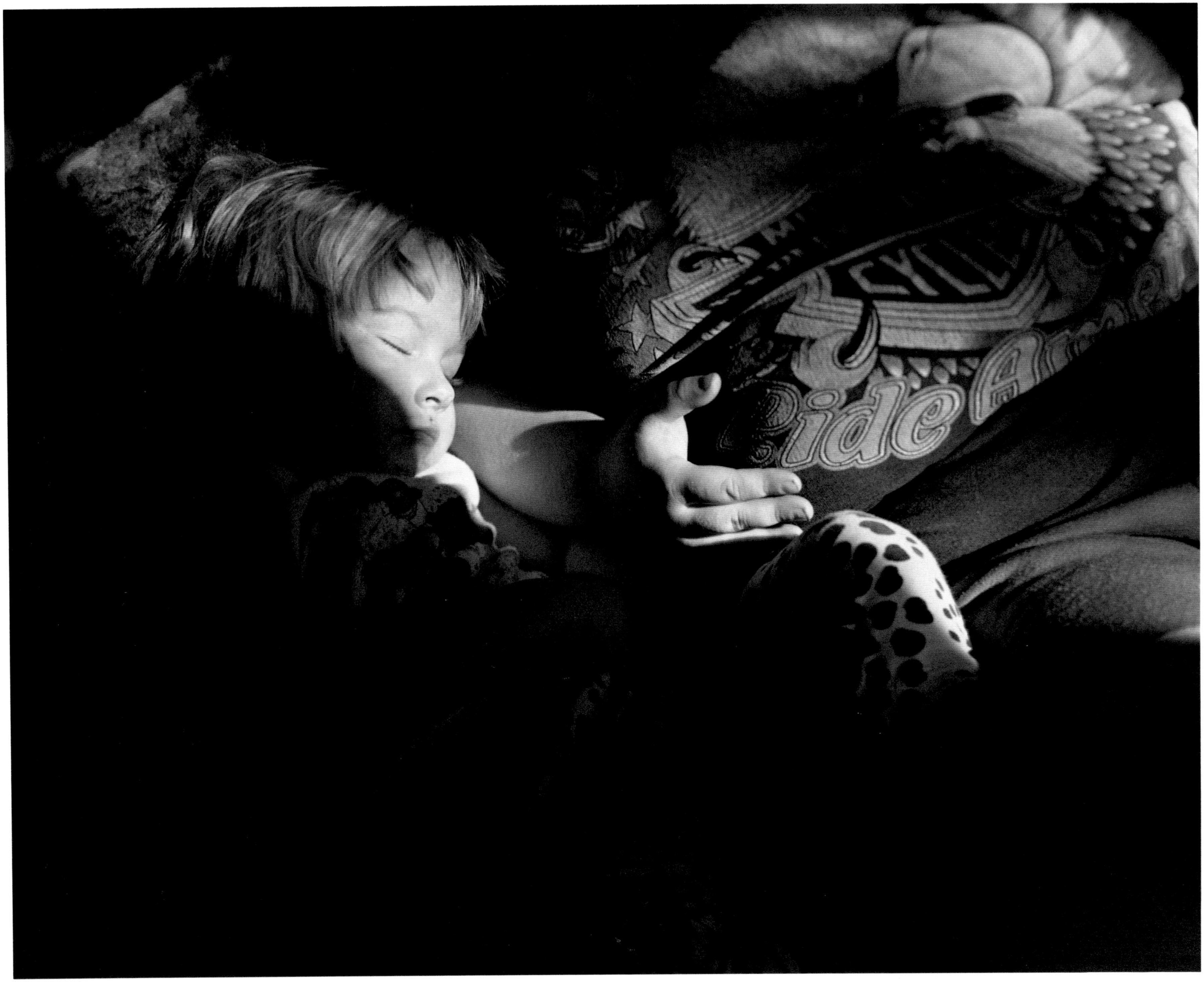

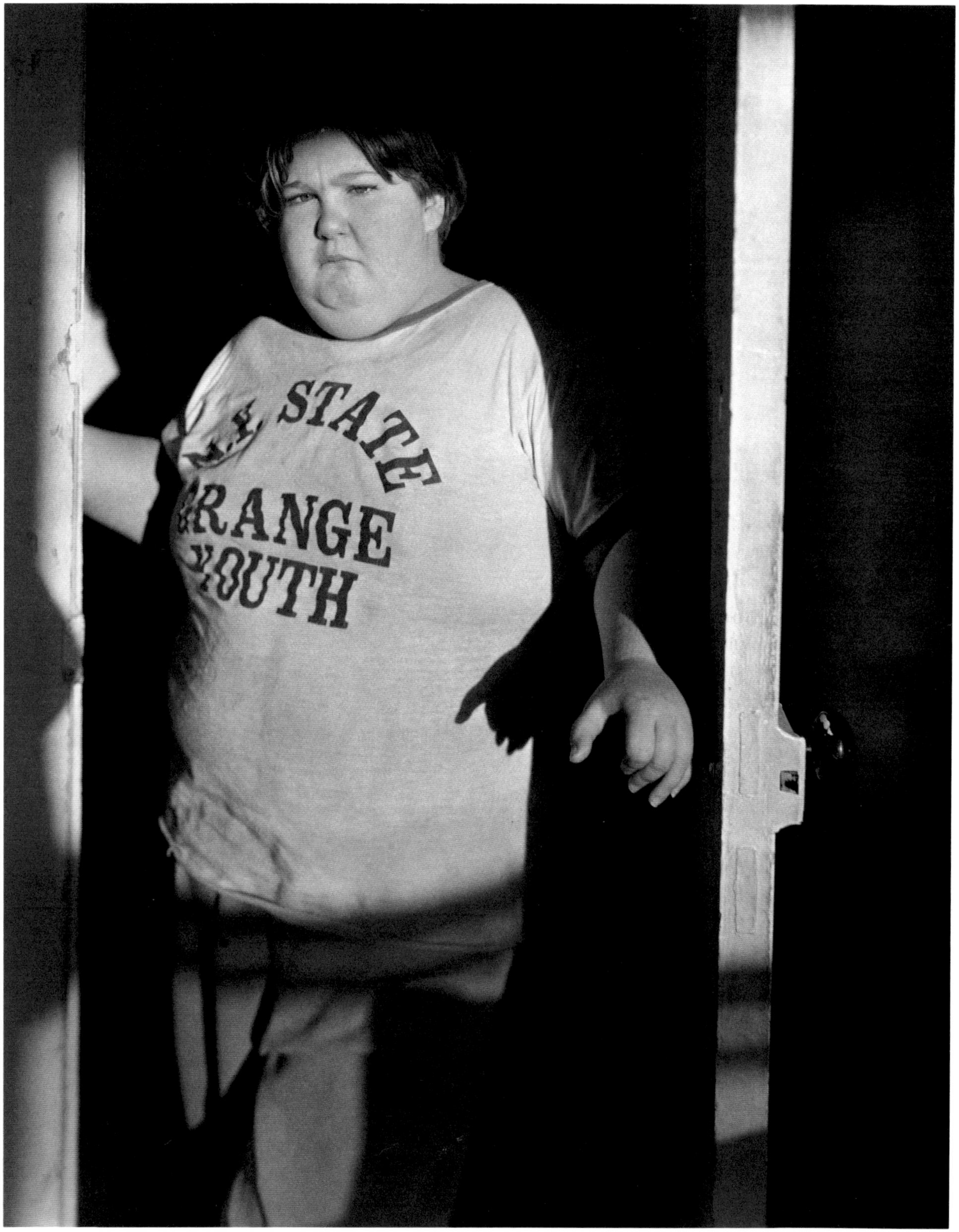
STATE

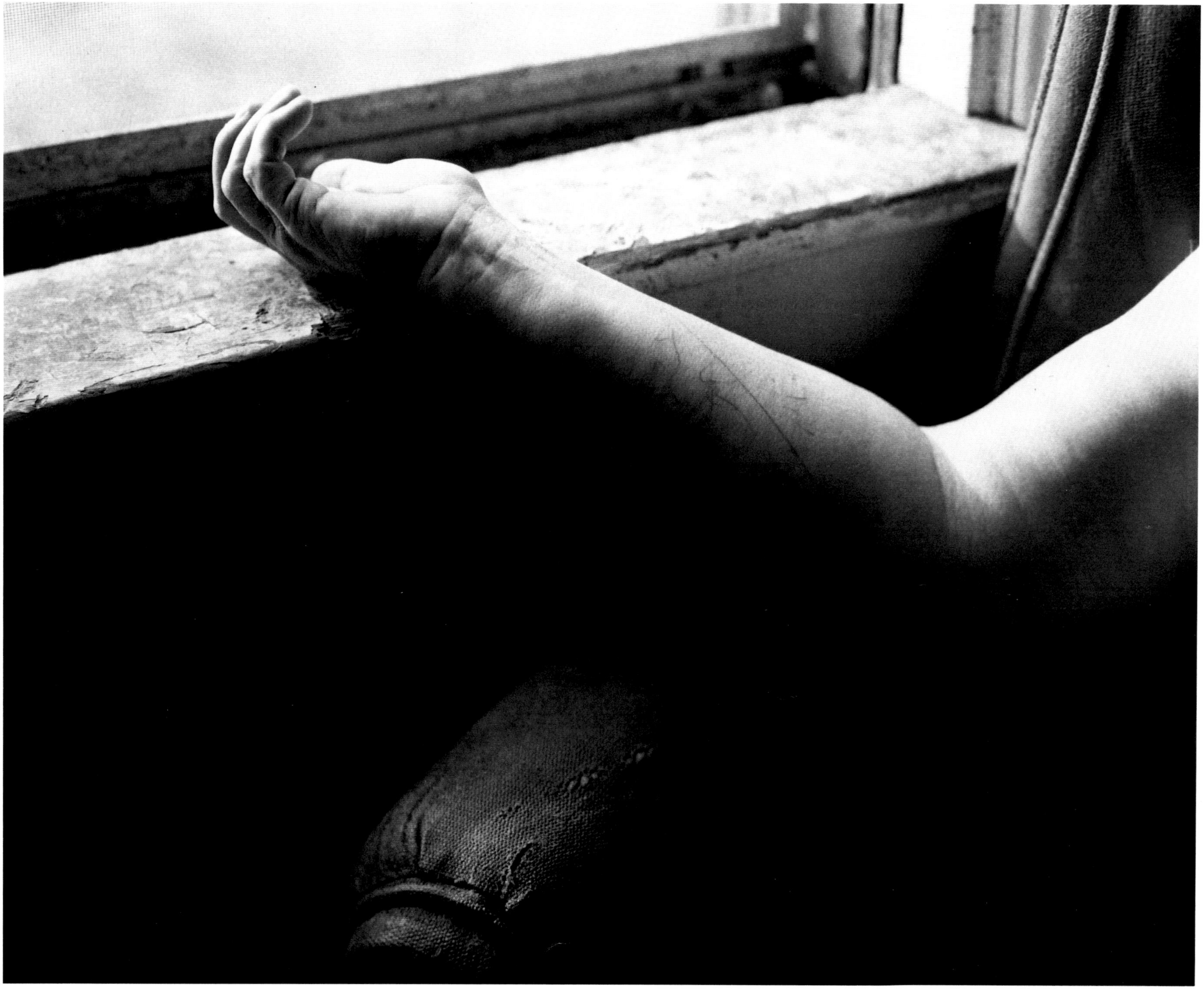

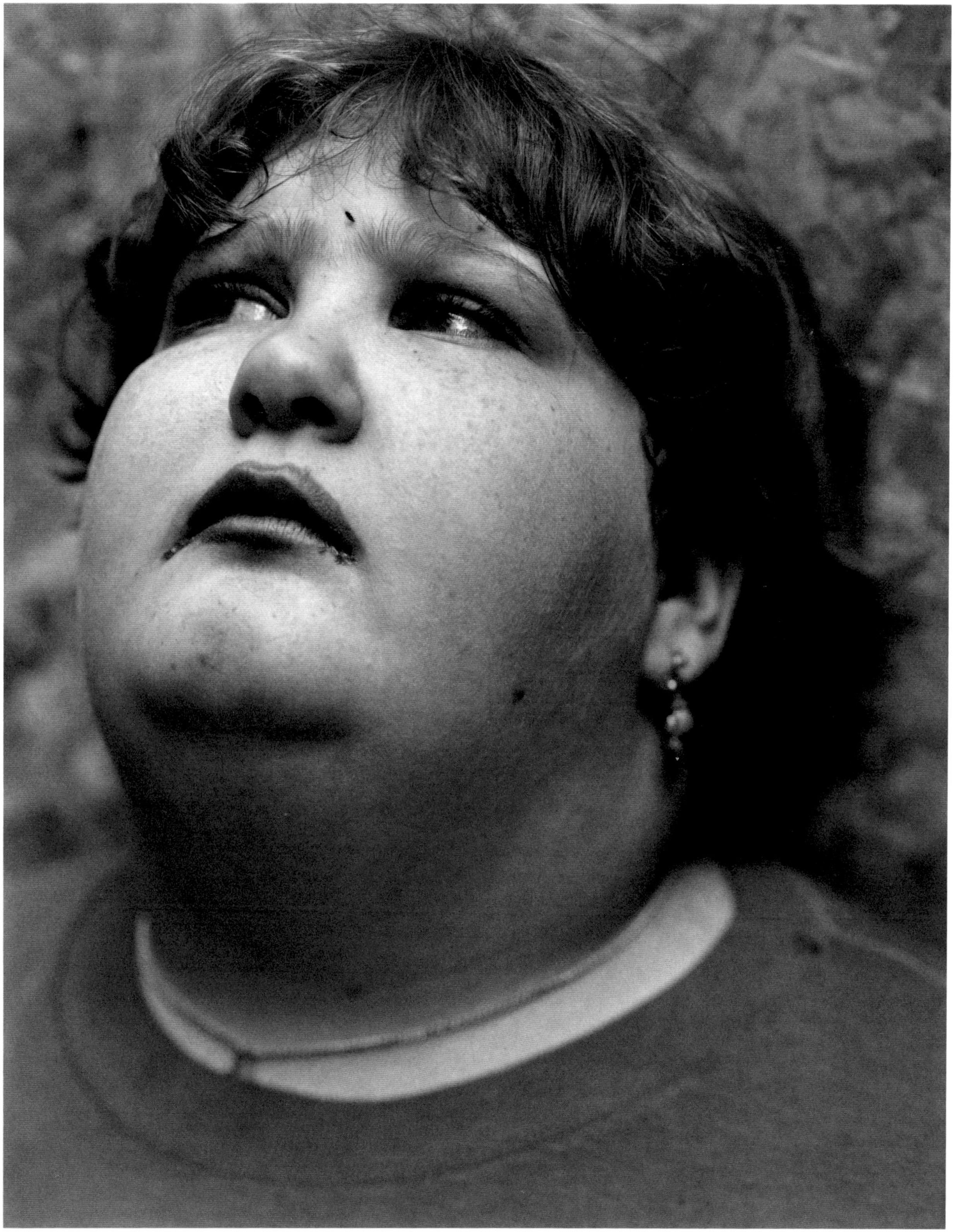

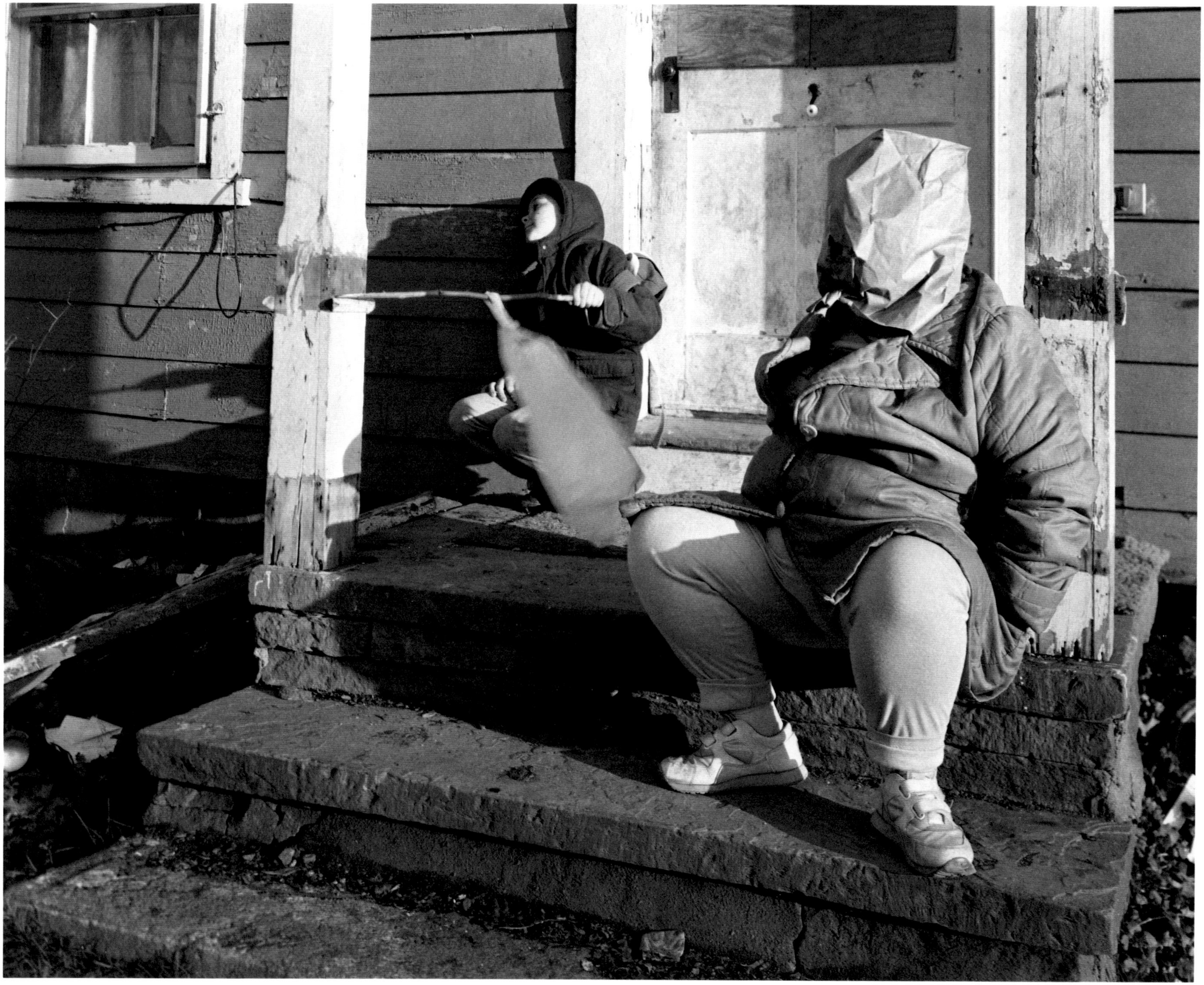

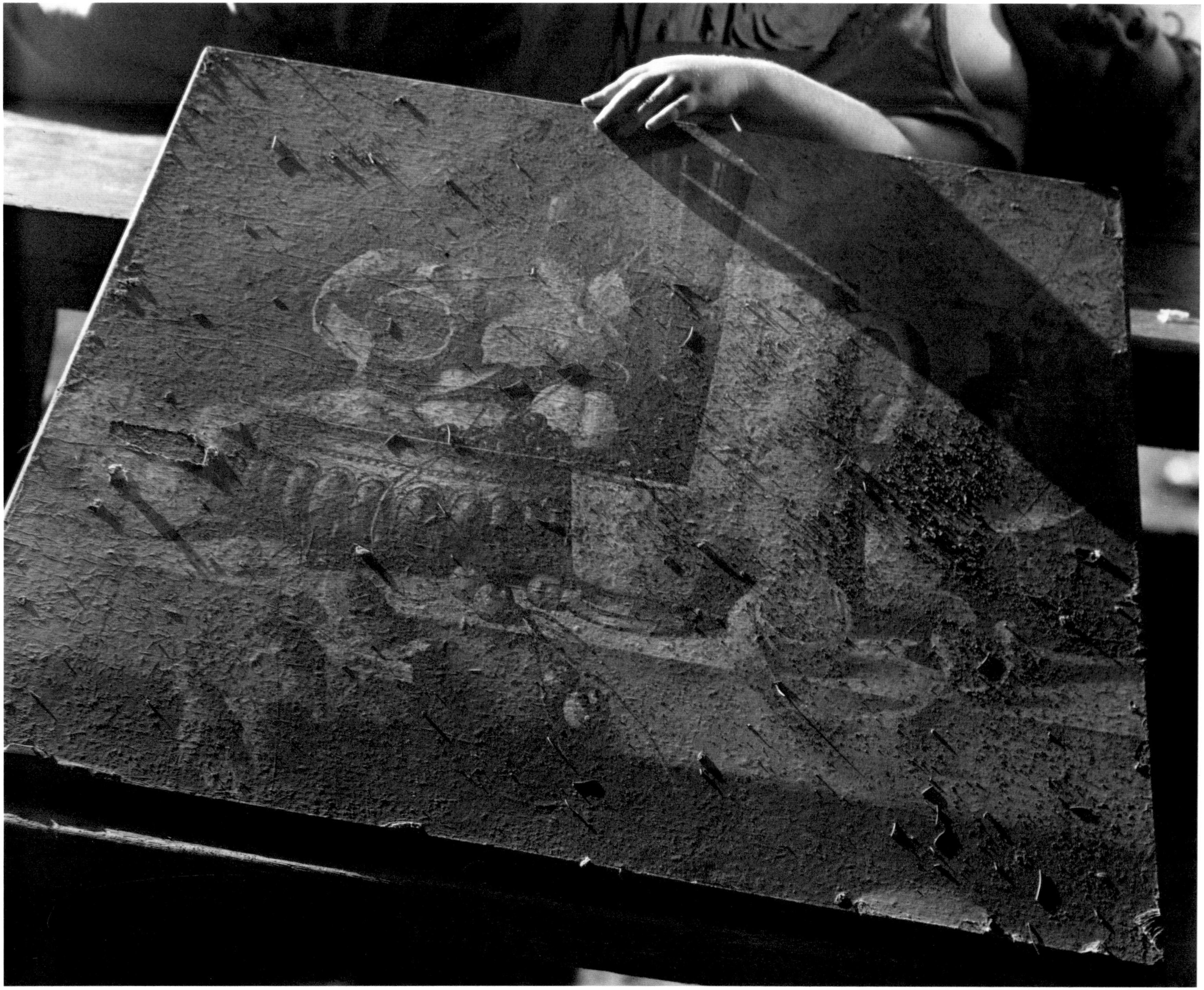

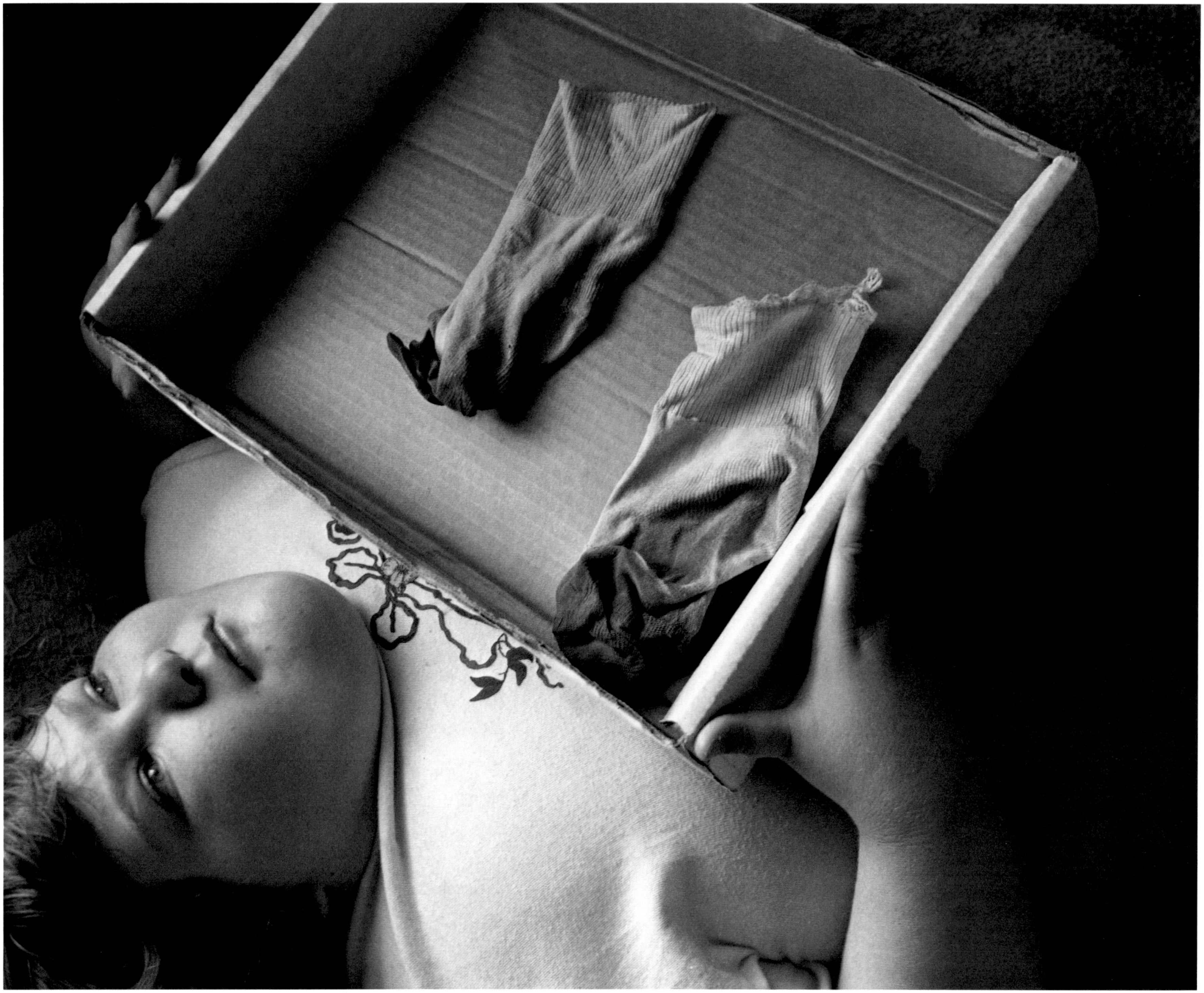

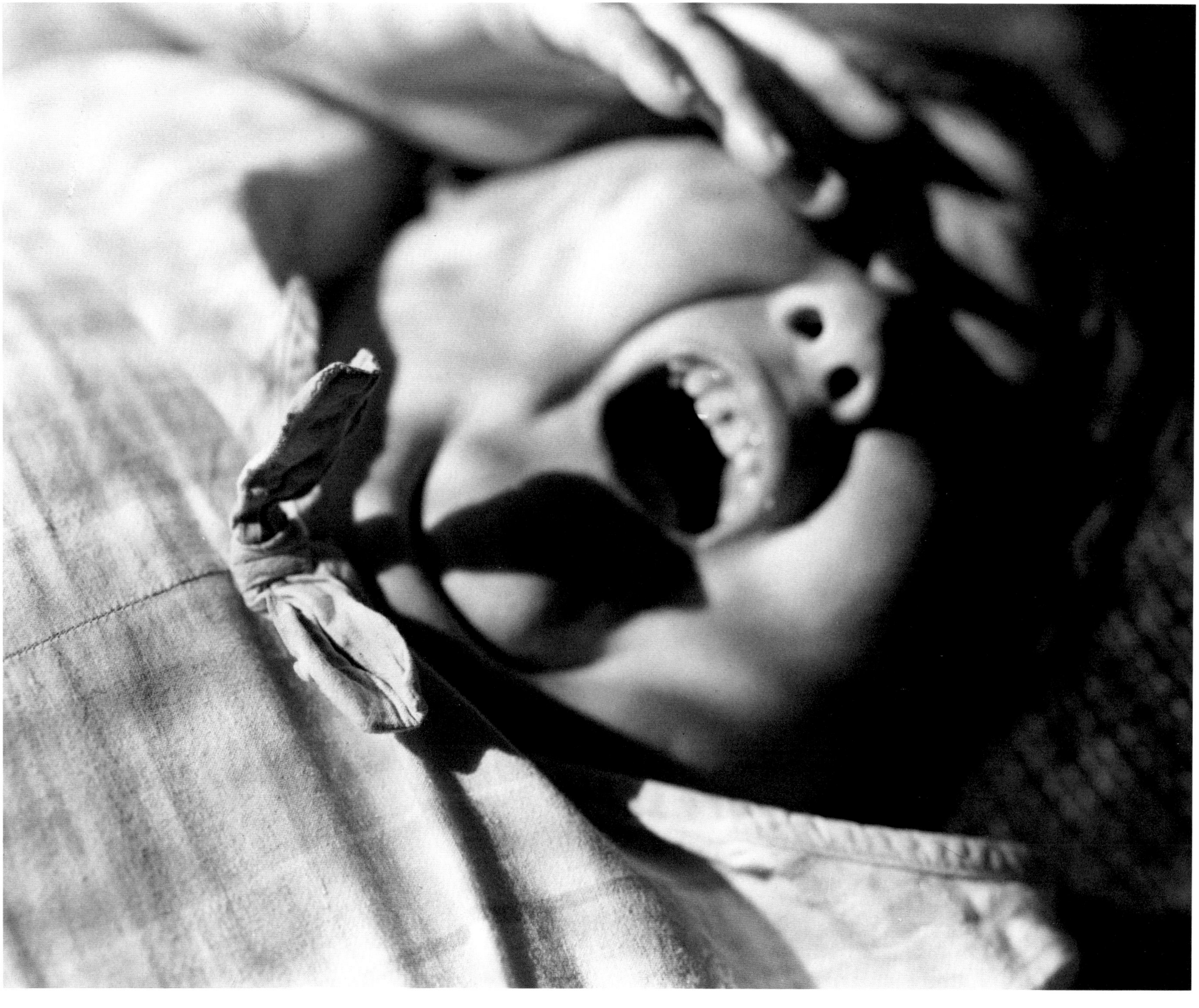

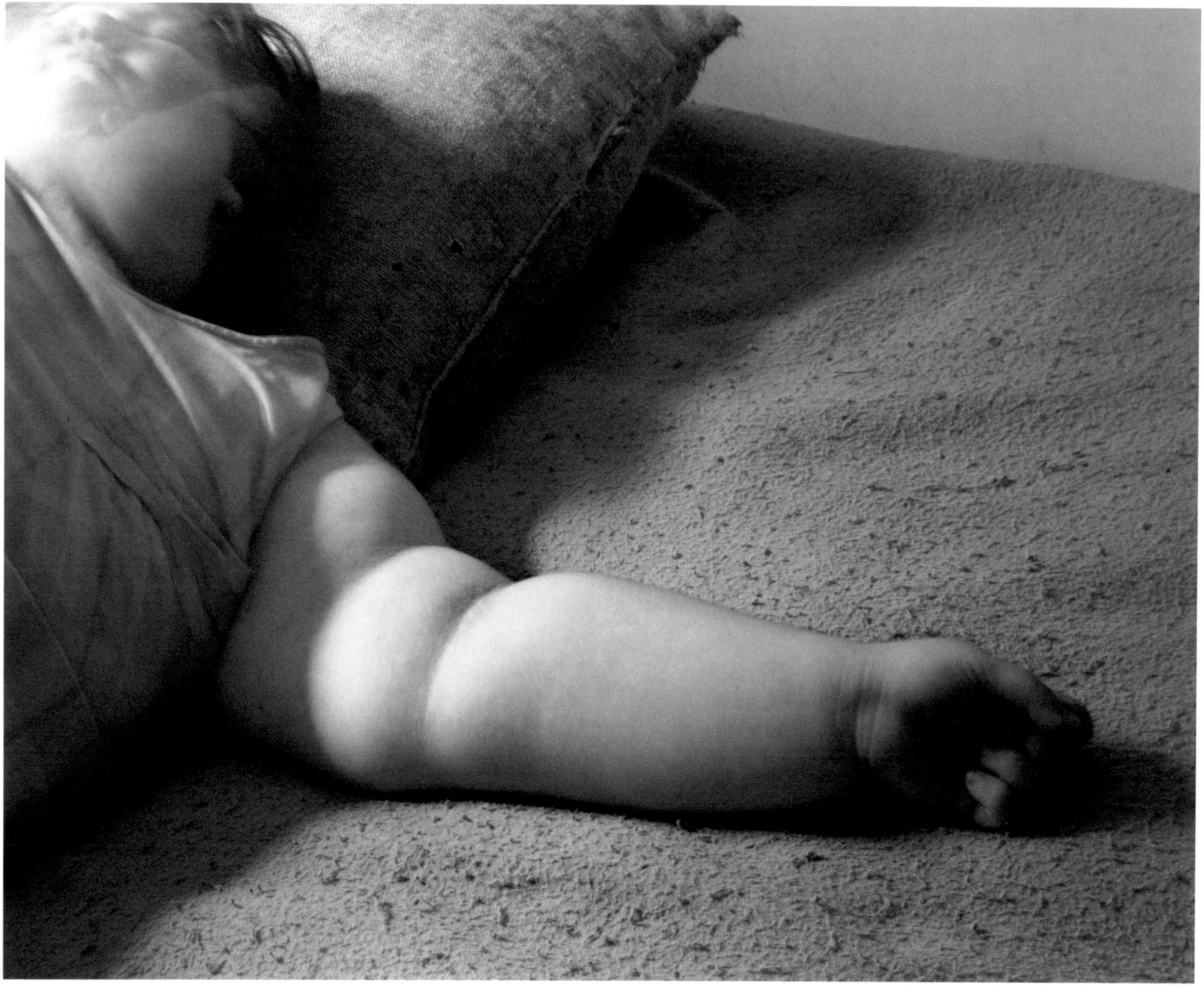

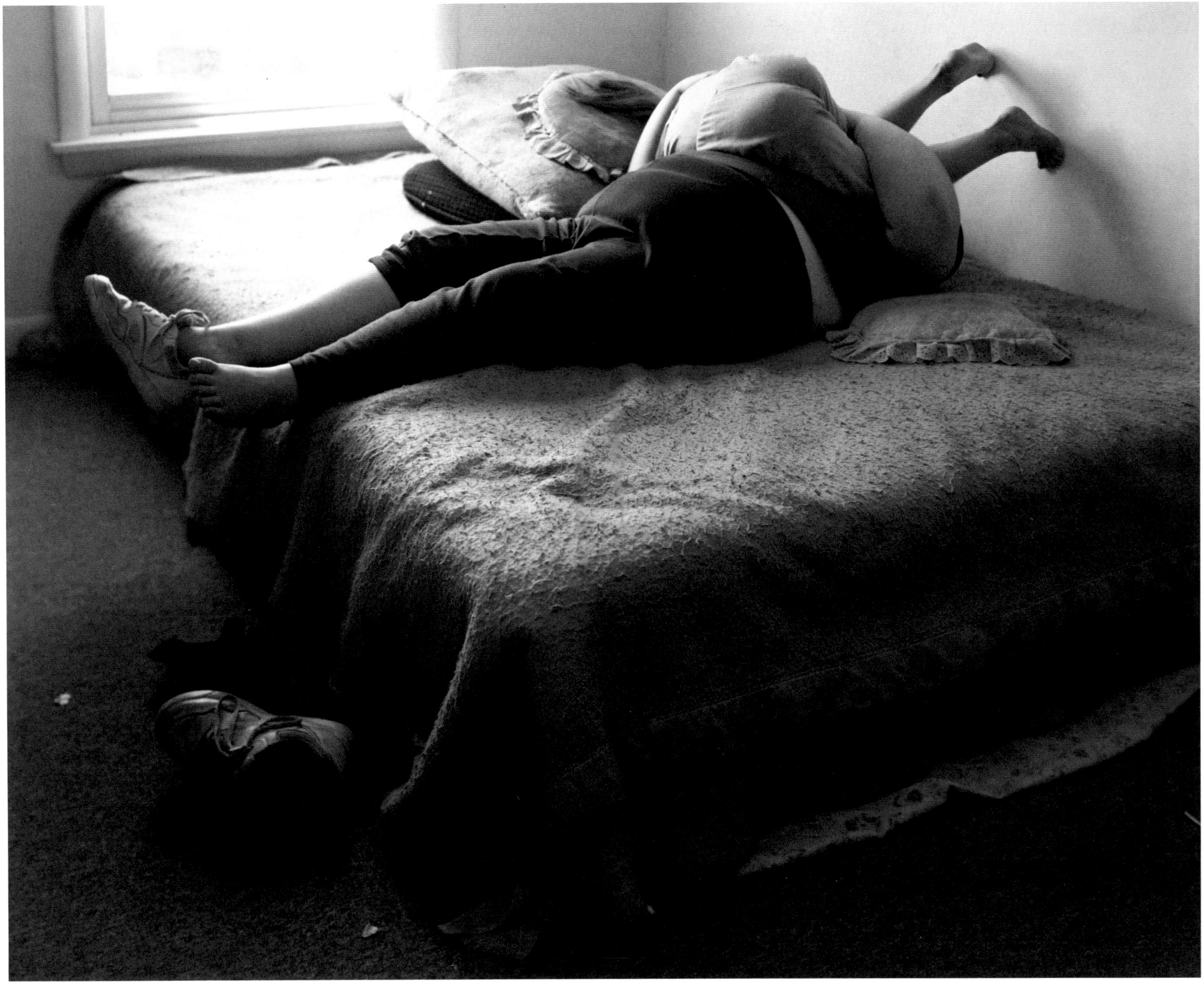

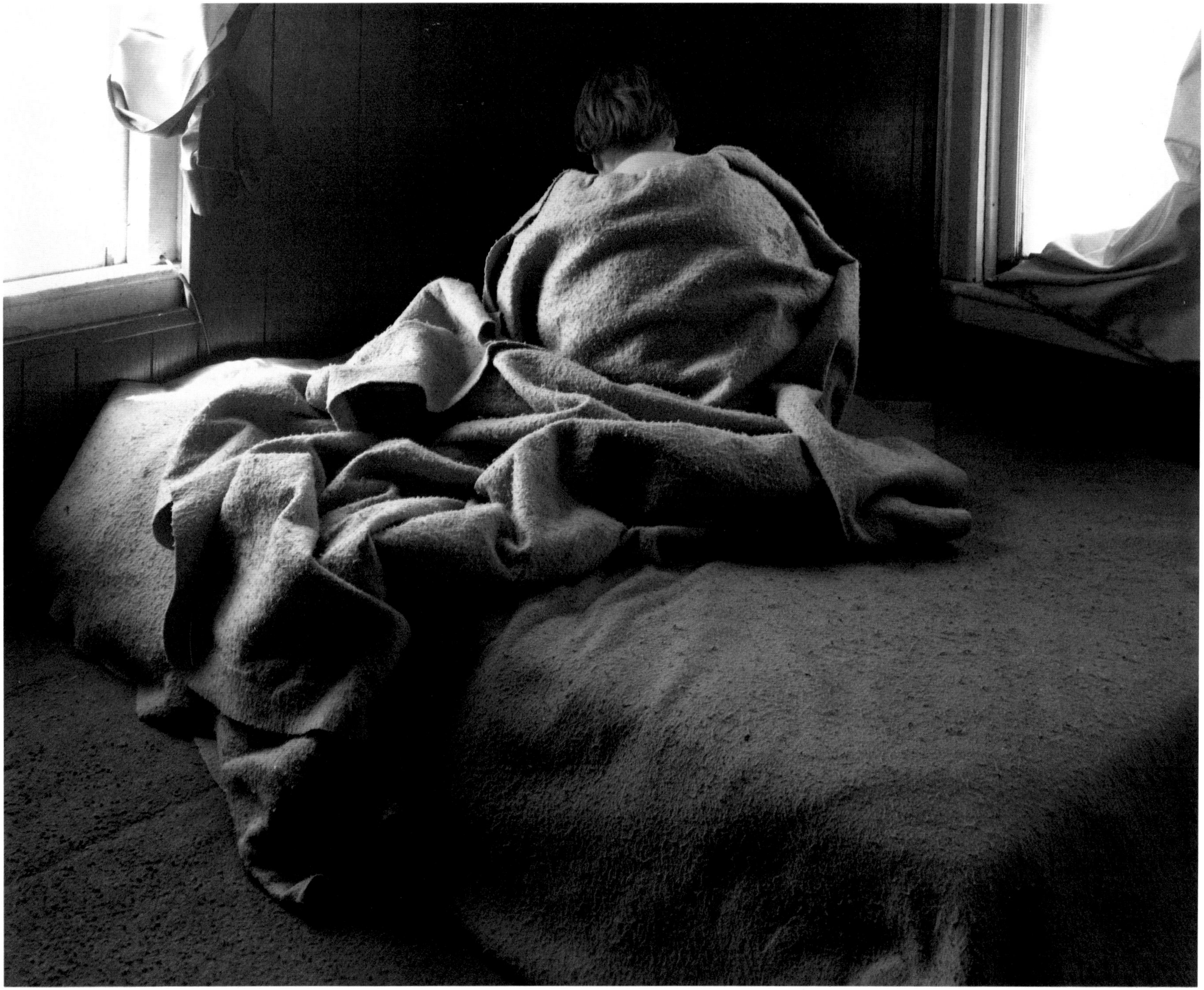

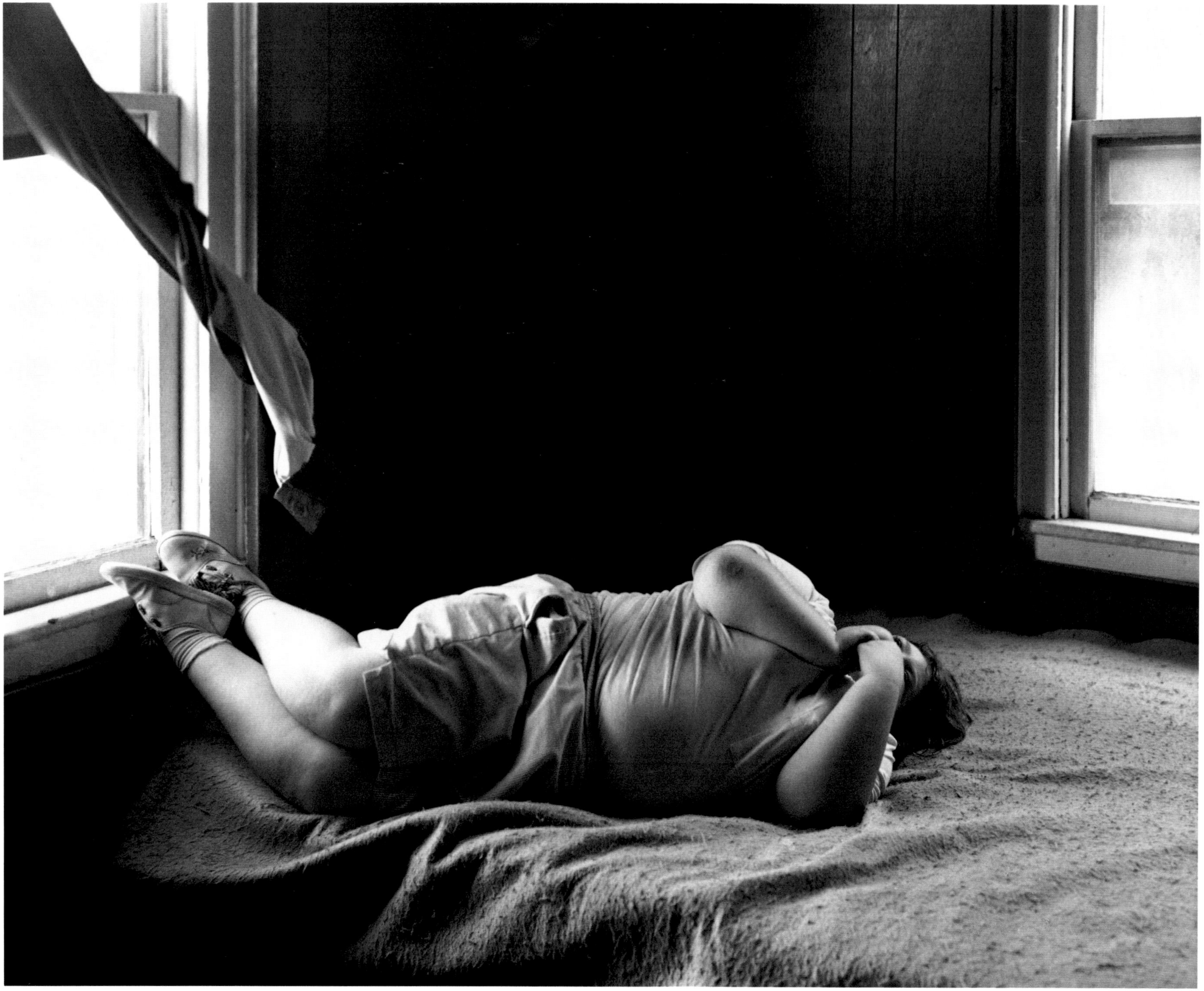

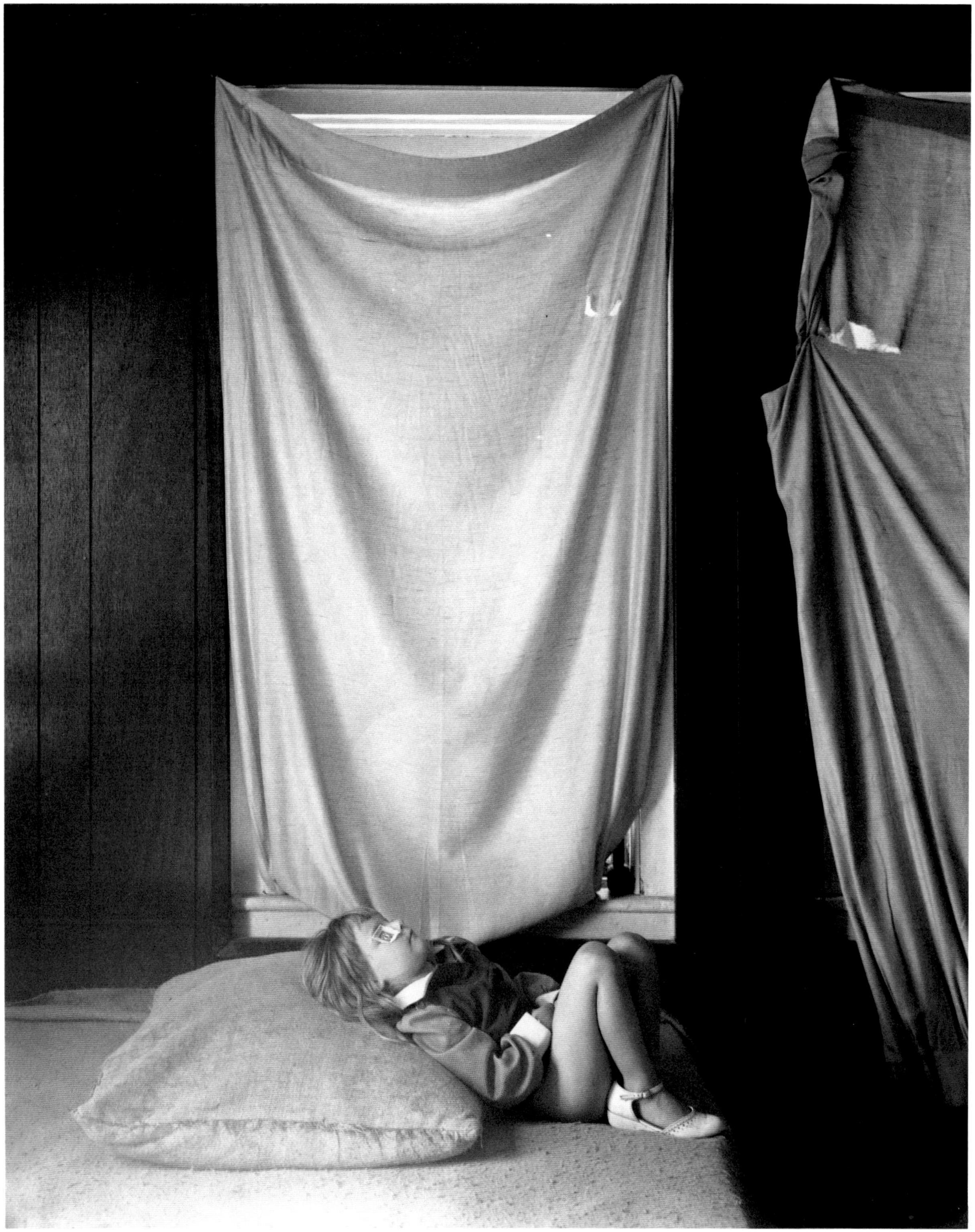

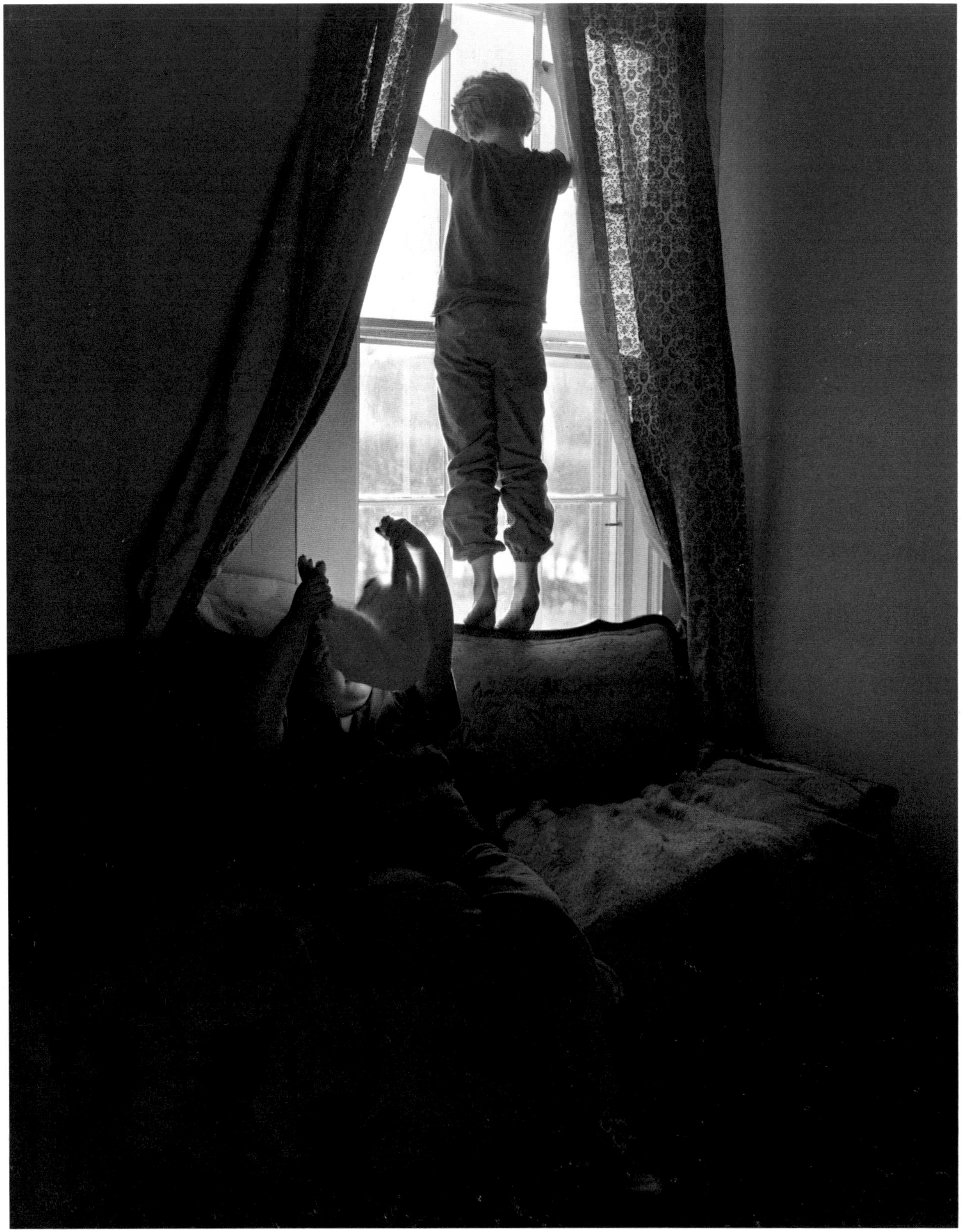

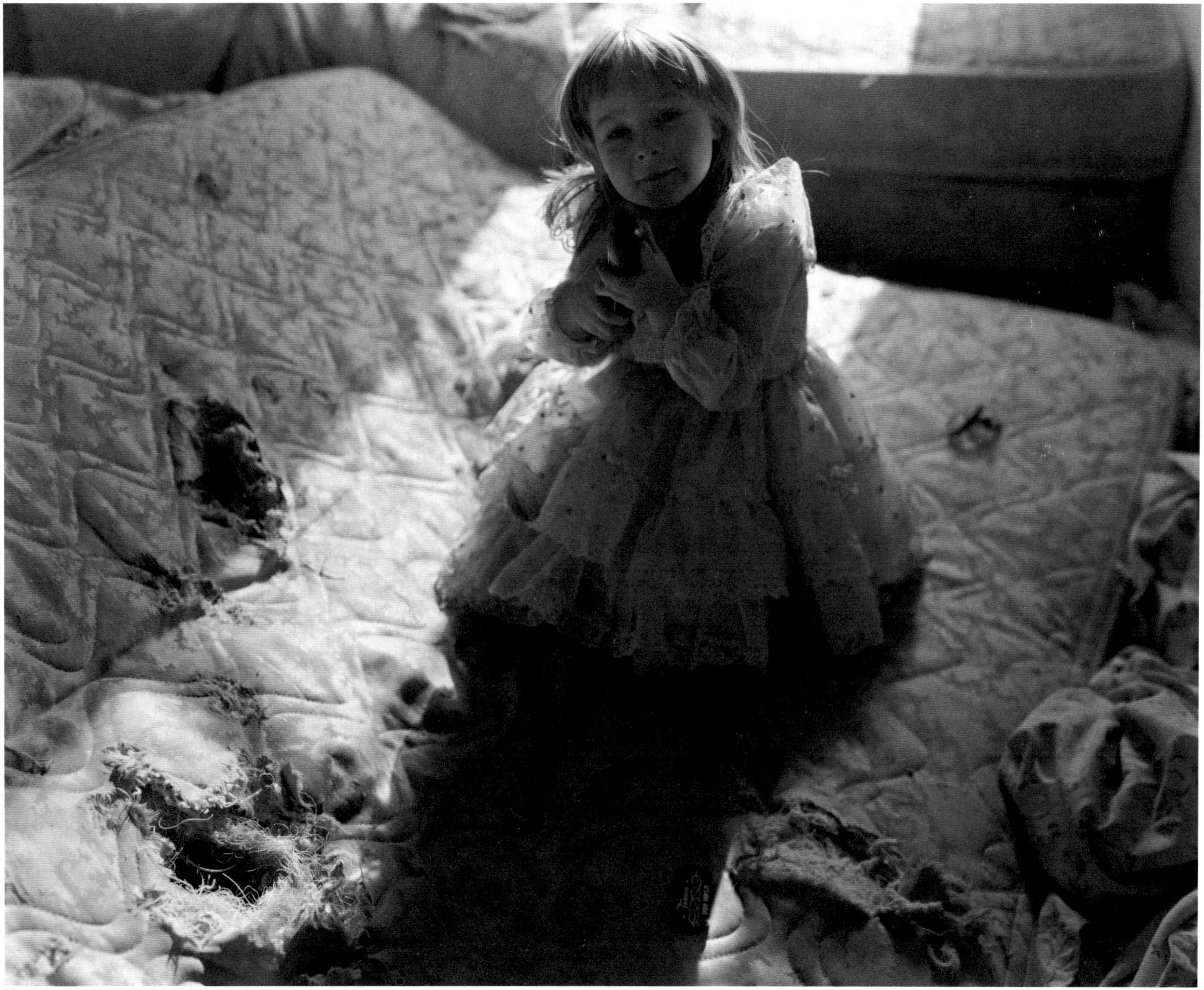

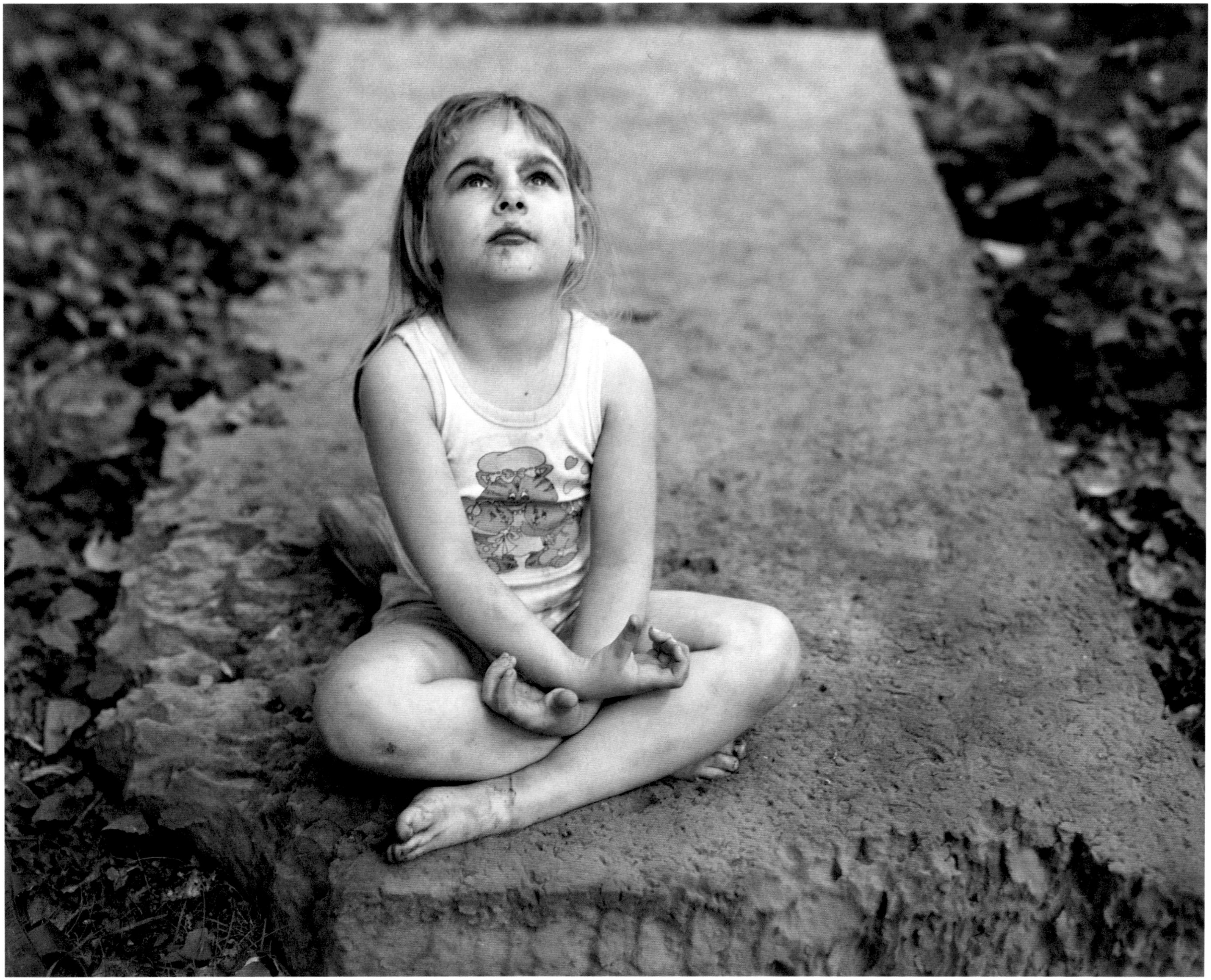

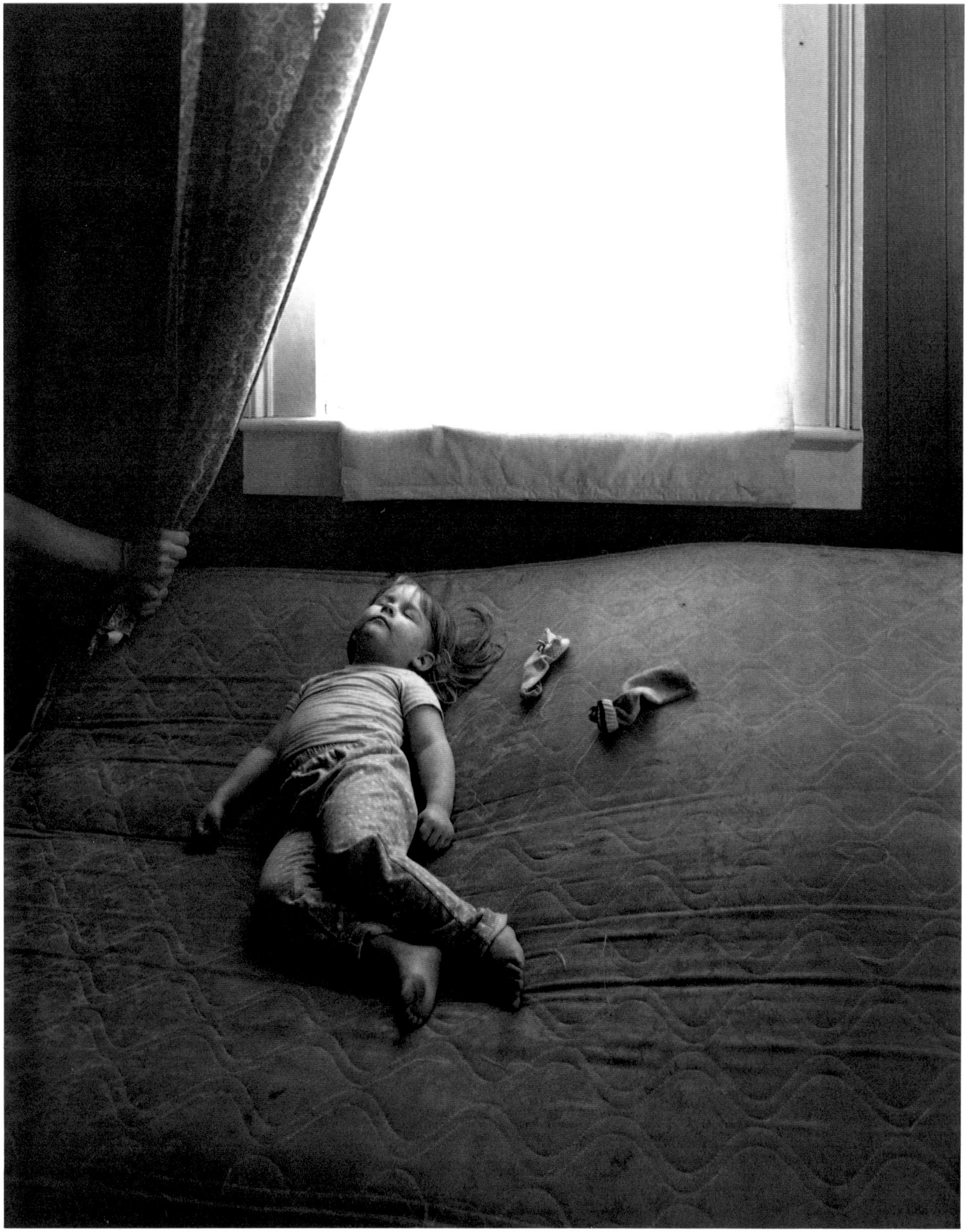

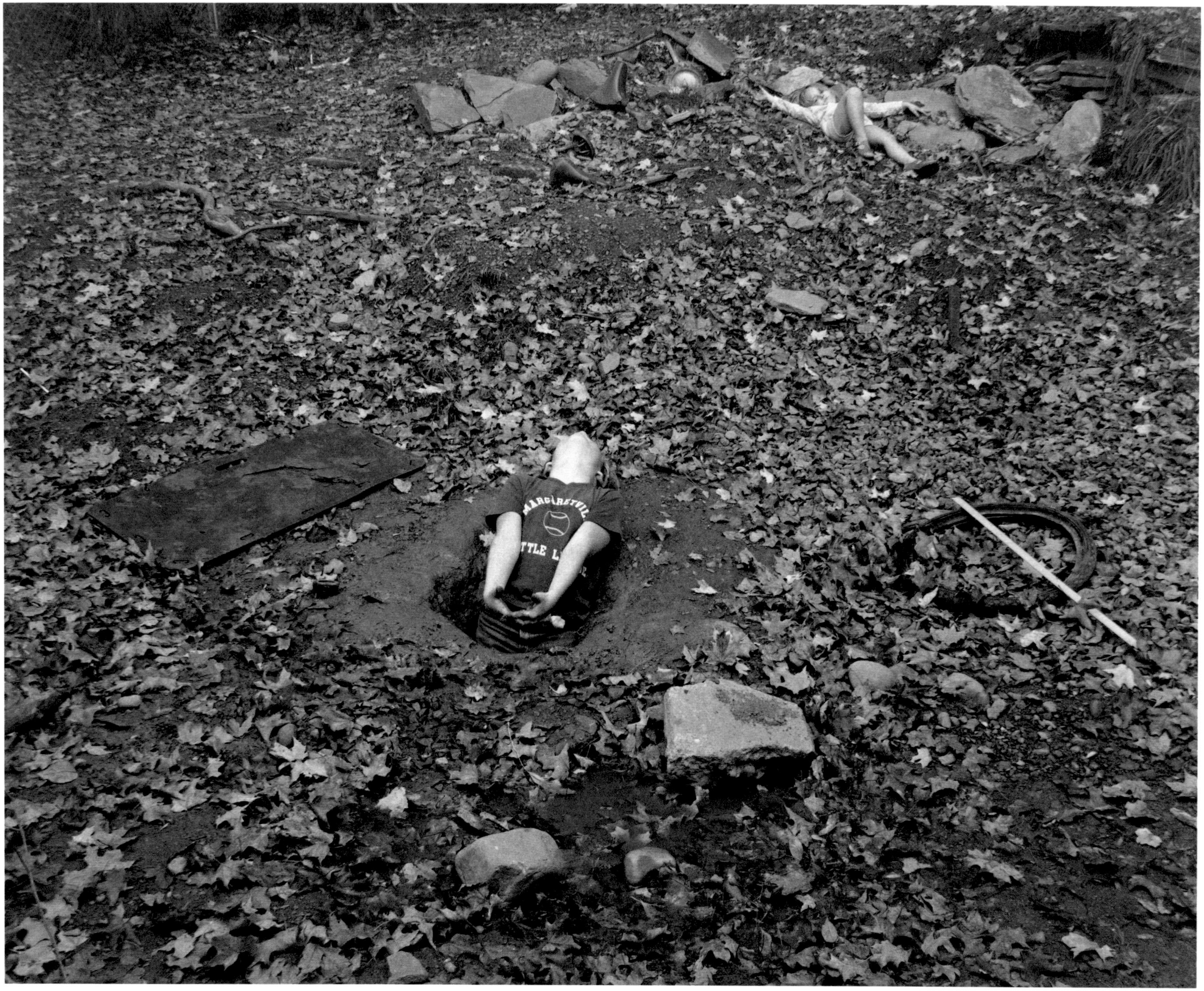

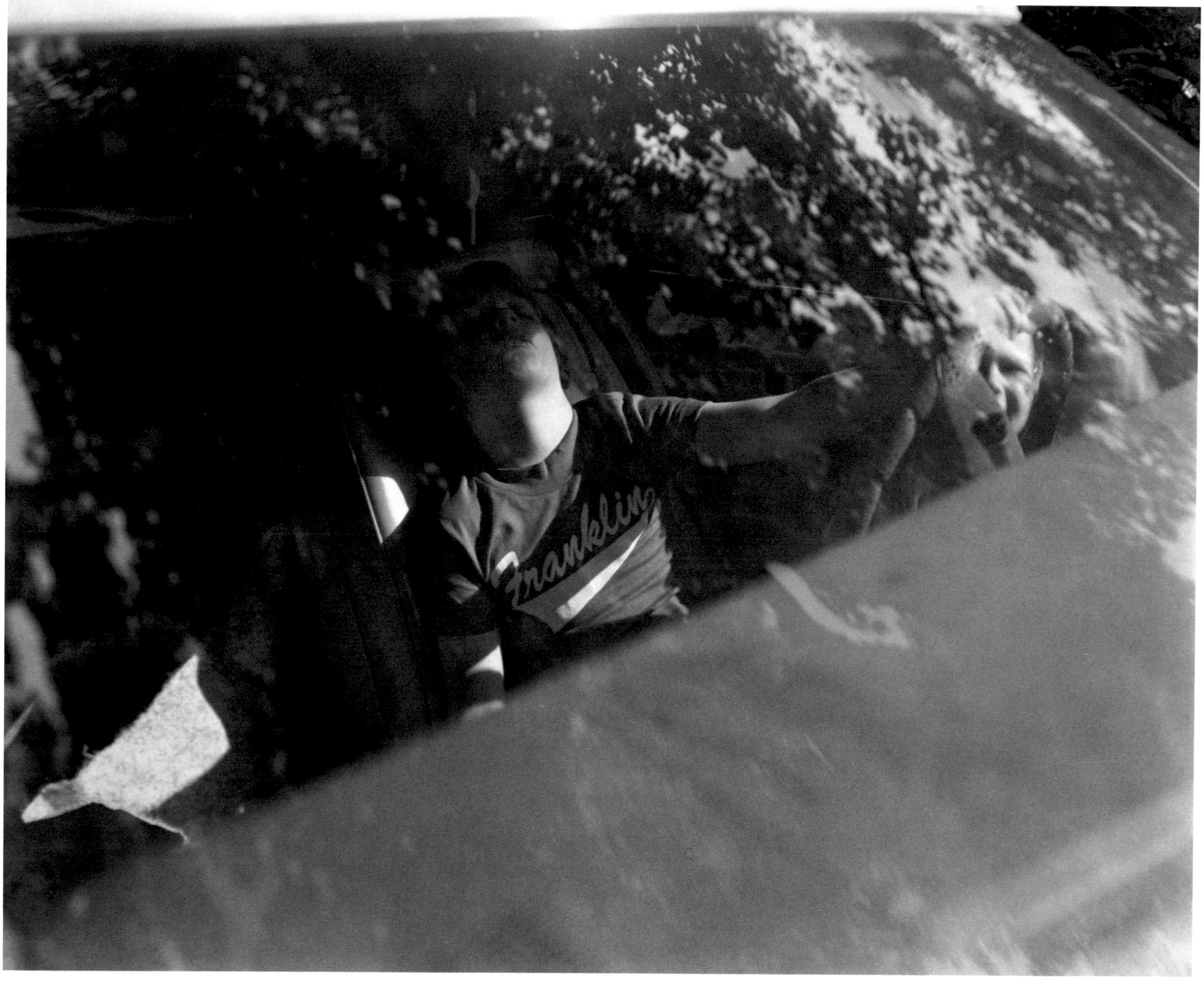
Franklin

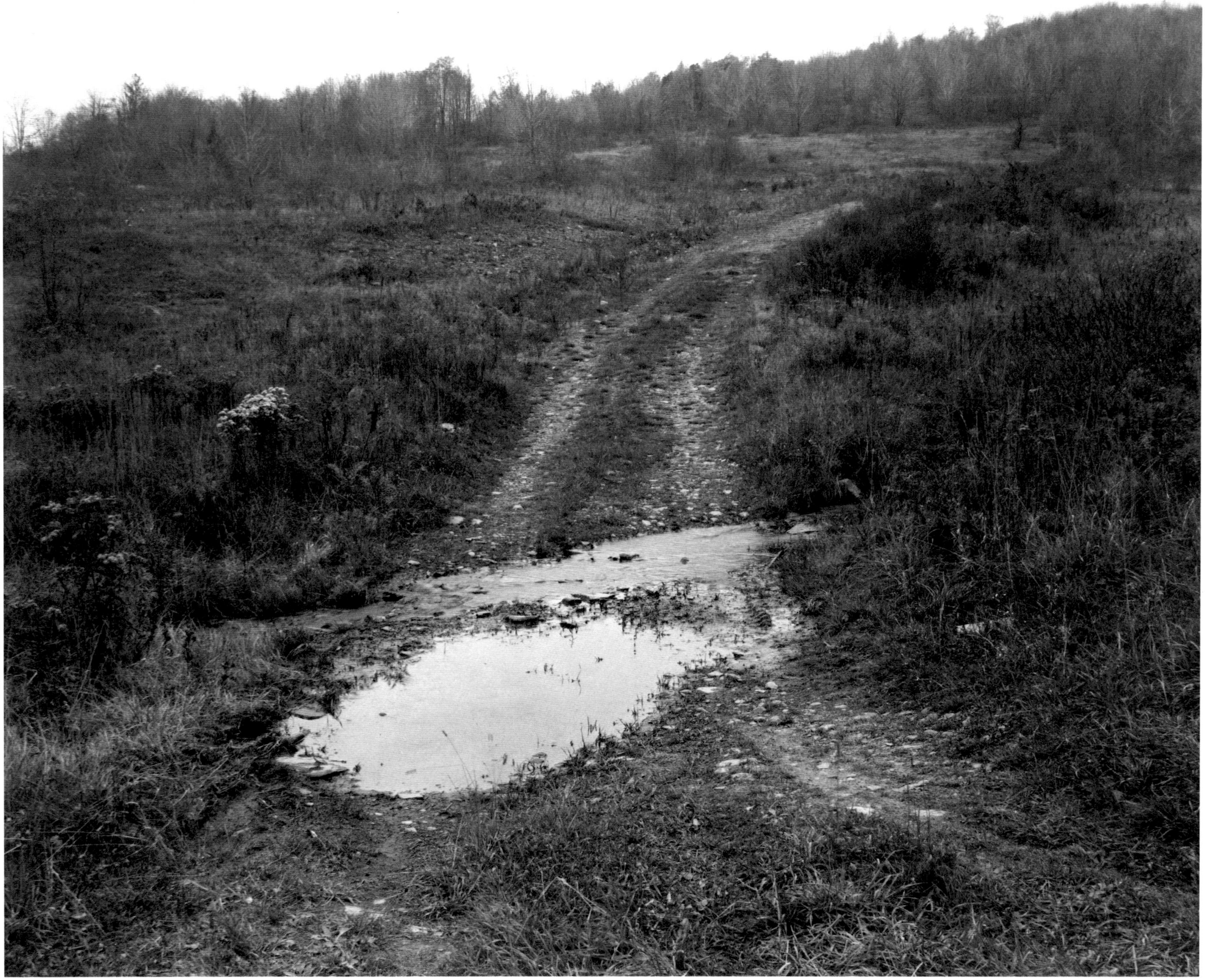

ACKNOWLEDGMENTS

I would like to thank Vince Aletti, Len Bellinger, Richard Benson, Lillian and Barbara Boecke, John Cohen, Lois Conner, Merry Foresta, Robert Hennessey, Paul and Wendy Kopeiken, Sally and Larry Mann, Maria Morris Hambourg, Tom Peters, Tod Papageorge, E. Annie Proulx, Will Stapp, Julie Saul, Connie Sullivan, Timothy Williams, and all the friends and family who have been supportive throughout the ten years of this project.

A. M.

The photographs in this book were made, in part, with support from the John Simon Guggenheim Foundation, the New York Foundation for the Arts, and the New York State Council on the Arts.

Produced by Constance Sullivan Editions

Design and typography by Tina Davis, New York

Duotone separations by Robert Hennessey

Printed by The Stinehour Press, Lunenburg, Vermont

Bound by Roswell Bookbinding Company, Phoenix, Arizona